# THE BATTLE
# OF BRITAIN

# RICHARD OVERY

# THE BATTLE

# OF BRITAIN

## The Myth and the Reality

**W. W. Norton & Company**

**New York    London**

First published in 2000 by Penguin Books Ltd.
Copyright © Richard Overy, 2000
First American edition 2001

Originally published in England under the title *The Battle*

Manufacturing by The Maple-Vail Book Manufacturing Group

Library of Congress Cataloging-in-Publication Data

Overy, R. J.
[Battle]
The Battle of Britain : the myth and the reality / by Richard Overy.
p. cm.
Originally published: The Battle. London : Penguin Books, c2000.
**ISBN 0-393-02008-8**
1. Britain, Battle of, 1940. I. Title.

D756.5.B7 O84 2000
940.54'211—dc21
00-069249

W. W. Norton  & Company, Inc., 500 Fifth Avenue, New York, N.Y. 10110
www.wwnorton.com

W. W. Norton & Company Ltd., 10 Coptic Street, London WC1A 1PU

1 2 3 4 5 6 7 8 9 0

# CONTENTS

# ACKNOWLEDGEMENTS

I would like to acknowledge the helpful assistance received in the Imperial War Museum, the Public Record Office, and above all in the Ministry of Defence, Air Historical Branch. I am particularly grateful to Sebastian Ritchie for casting an expert eye over the text at very short notice. Simon Winder at Penguin was the inspiration behind the subject and its format. Kate Parker has been a scrupulous editor. Any errors and misjudgements that remain are, as ever, my own responsibility. To Kim, Alexandra and Clementine my love and thanks.

# PREFACE

For sixty years 'The Battle' has meant one thing to the British people: the Battle of Britain. The contest between the British and German air forces in the late summer and autumn of 1940 has become a defining moment in our recent history, as Trafalgar was for the Victorians. British forces fought other great battles in the twentieth century – the Somme, Passchendaele, Normandy – but only El Alamein exudes the same sweet scent of complete victory, and Egypt was not the Motherland.

In reality neither El Alamein nor the Battle of Britain was a clear-cut battle with a neat conclusion. This has not stopped historians from imposing clarity, nor has it dulled the popular perception that these were glittering milestones along the road to British military success. Both battles were really defensive triumphs: the one saved Egypt and prevented the collapse of Britain's global war effort, the other saved Britain from cheap conquest. It is avoiding defeat that we have applauded; victory came long afterwards, with more powerful allies in harness.

'The Battle' matters because it prevented German invasion and conquest and kept Britain in the war. This achievement was worthwhile enough. Nine European states (ten, counting Danzig) had failed to prevent German occupation by the summer of 1940, with the grimmest of consequences. Nevertheless, some historians have raised serious doubts about the traditional story of the battle, which gave birth to the myth of a united nation repelling invasion, and gave iconographic status to the Spitfires and the 'few' who flew them. There is another history to be discovered behind the popular narrative. The effort to uncover it has already challenged some of the most cherished illusions of the battle story.

Take, for example, the generally accepted view that the battle prevented German invasion of southern Britain. Documents on the German side have been used to suggest that this was not so. Invasion, it can be argued, was a bluff designed to force Britain to beg for peace; in the summer of 1940 Hitler's eyes were already gazing eastwards, where there lay real 'living-space'. The Royal Air

Force did not repel invasion for the apparently simple reason that the Germans were never coming. This interpretation has prompted some historians to suggest that Britain should have taken the chance of peace with Hitler and let the two totalitarian states bleed each other to death in eastern Europe.

Behind this argument lies still more revision. The picture of a firmly united and determined people standing shoulder to shoulder against fascism has been slowly eroded by the weight of historical evidence. The British were less united in 1940 than was once universally believed. Defeatism could be found, side by side with heroic defiance. Churchill's government, so it is argued, had powerful voices urging a search for peace in the summer of 1940, just like the appeasers of the 1930s. Churchill himself has not been free of reassessment. He has become the butt of wide criticism for his conduct of the war and his style of leadership. Even his inspirational speeches, which have shaped our memory of that summer of 1940, can now be shown to have had a mixed reception among a public desperate for hard news.

It is the purpose of this short book to assess where 'The Battle' now stands in history. There is little point in pretending that the historical narrative of the battle is the same as the popular myth. But it is not necessarily the case that the significance of the battle is diminished by recreating the historical reality, any more than the effects of Churchill's leadership must be negated by acknowledging that he was human too. For a great many reasons the Battle of Britain, myth and reality, was a necessary battle. The consequences of British abdication in 1940 would have been a calamity not just for the British people but for the world as a whole.

# ONE THE SETTING

We have reason to believe that Germany will be ruthless and indiscriminate in her endeavour to paralyse and destroy our national effort and morale and unless immediate steps are taken to reduce the intensity of attack it is conceivable that the enemy may achieve her object.

**Air Ministry memorandum, April 1938**[1]

For most of the 1930s Britain's politicians and military leaders were haunted by nightmare visions of a massive 'knock-out blow' from the air against which there could be little defence save the threat of retaliation. When Neville Chamberlain, Britain's prime minister from 1937 to 1940, flew back to London from Germany at the height of the Czech crisis in 1938, he looked down at the sprawling suburbs of the capital and imagined bombs crashing down upon the innocent victims below him. This horrible picture inspired him to redouble his efforts for peace. A year later, on 3 September, those efforts were finally undone. Britain declared war on Germany for her refusal to withdraw invasion forces from Poland, whose sovereignty Chamberlain had guaranteed five months before.

Almost immediately after Chamberlain broadcast the news from 10 Downing Street that Britain was at war, the sirens sounded. No one had told Chamberlain about the possibility of an air raid and he was 'visibly shaken' by it. It was a false alarm. A second one sounded at 3 a.m. that night, getting all London out of bed. For days people waited for the blow from the air which they had been told to expect. Government observers reported that 70 per cent of Londoners carried their gas masks with them.[2] The blow never came. The German Air Force had no plans to bomb London in 1939. Like the Royal Air Force (RAF), it was under strict instructions not to start the bombing war or to run the risk of killing civilians from the air. By the end of March only 1 per cent of Londoners could be seen carrying gas masks.

The war the British waged in 1939 was very different from the one they had expected to fight. Chamberlain's government poured millions of pounds into air power between 1937 and 1939 in order to provide a defensive shield against the knock-out blow, a defence made possible thanks to the fast monoplane fighter and the invention of radar. Millions more went into the expansion of Bomber Command as a deterrent against air attack. Plans were drawn up to bomb the enemy if he would not be deterred. The civilian population was drilled in air-raid precautions so as to reduce the colossal casualties predicted from all-out air war. Much of the top-level thinking on future war presupposed that something like the Battle of Britain might well occur in its very early stages, perhaps without a declaration of war at all.

In Germany the air force took a less extravagant view of air power. There the emphasis lay on combined operations with the army in order to impose a decisive defeat on enemy armed forces. This was and always had been a central principle of German war-making. German air leaders certainly possessed by 1939 the technical means to create an operationally independent air force for long-range attacks on industrial sectors or civilian morale. It was not moral scruple that held them back. They simply did not believe that these were strategically desirable targets. Neither promised immediate results given the nature of current air technology; neither would necessarily bring the enemy armed forces any closer to defeat. The manual for 'The Conduct of Air Warfare' first drawn up in 1936, and revised in March 1940, directed German air fleets to seek out the enemy air and ground forces and inflict upon them debilitating blows. Joint manoeuvres carried out with the army from 1935 onwards showed what could be achieved when armies and air forces fought together. The proof was supplied in the swift demolition of Polish resistance in September 1939. When planning began for the next campaign against Britain and France, it was based on the same formula of fast, hard-hitting air and armoured forces, designed to win a swift battle of annihilation. What were defined as 'terror attacks' against civilian targets far from the scene of battle were to be permitted only in retaliation for terror attacks by the enemy.[3]

The British were largely unprepared for this kind of warfare. Until February 1939, when Chamberlain publicly pledged British military support for France, Britain did not even have a Continental ally to consider. British strategy in the 1930s was insular. The government's first priority was the protection of the British imperial heartland, even if this meant starving the global empire of adequate resources for its defence. Hence the decision, taken when British rearmament began in earnest in 1936, to allocate the lion's share of resources to the Royal Air Force and the Royal Navy. Britain's offensive capability remained dangerously underdeveloped. Even by 1939 only two fully equipped divisions were available immediately to fight in Europe; Bomber Command, the much-vaunted striking arm of the RAF, had fewer than 500 aircraft when war broke out, incapable of reaching very far into German territory. British preparations had been based on the narrow objective of avoiding defeat and conquest. This was scarcely the state of mind necessary to conduct a major land campaign in Europe.

The fundamental ambiguity at the heart of British military preparations explains the flawed response to the demands of coalition warfare. There was little the British could do to help Poland. Assistance to France was compromised by the small scale of the army Britain sent, and by an unwillingness to commit to the land campaign aircraft that had been assigned to Britain's own defence. The aircraft that were sent out to make up the British Advanced Air Striking Force (an organization only a little larger than the Polish Air Force, which German aviators had snuffed out in a few days) were rendered ineffective by the poor state of Allied communications and the French insistence that aircraft fight a short-range, army co-operation role to which the RAF had given almost no serious thought.

When the attack on France came on 10 May 1940, these deficiencies were soon exposed. There was often a lapse of four or five hours between sighting a fleeting battlefield target and the despatch of instructions for aircraft to attack it. British bombers in France (most of them light Battle and Blenheim aircraft, which were utterly out-classed in daylight combat) had to wait for orders to be routed from France, through Bomber Command head-quarters near London, and back again to France.[4] Co-operation with the army was rudimentary. While 380 dive-bombers gave close air support to advancing German troops, often reacting within minutes of a radioed request, the RAF managed between September 1939 and March 1940 to train a mere seven pilots in dive-bombing techniques, who between them dropped just 56 bombs in practice. When the French asked the RAF what Bomber Command could do to interrupt the remorseless progress of German forces, they were told that the most they could expect was the temporary disruption of three railway lines.[5]

The only serious contribution made by the RAF came with the deployment of squadrons of Hurricane fighters, which had been intended for Britain's own defence. As the battle in France deepened during May 1940, more and more Hurricanes had to be sent in piecemeal to stem the haemorrhage of Allied air power. Without the home advantages of prepared bases and radar warning, fighter losses were high. In May and June, 477 fighters were destroyed and 284 pilots killed, rates of loss not far short of those later in the summer. So severe was the drain on home defence that the commander-in-chief of Fighter Command, Sir Hugh Dowding, took the unprecedented step of talking directly to the War Cabinet on 15 May to plead for restraint. 'I saw my resources slipping away,' he later wrote, 'like sand in an hourglass.'[6] The politicians only half responded to his argument. Churchill insisted on sending further Hurricanes, but the French got none of the coveted high-performance Spitfires. Only when British forces were pinned back on Dunkirk and faced with annihilation in the last week of May did the RAF get drawn into the battle in strength. Flying from bases in southern Britain, at the limit of their range, they established brief periods of air superiority over the beaches, and inflicted 132 aircraft losses on the German Air Force in three days of fighting. Spitfires were used in this later phase of the battle in France, but 155 of them were lost, 65 of them in accidents as aircrew tried to master the new equipment. The Dunkirk evacuation was the starting point of almost a year of continuous air combat for the defence of Britain.[7]

The contest that Britain faced after Dunkirk was the war Britain had expected. It was in effect to be a 'Chamberlain war', for this was the kind of defensive conflict he had anticipated and prepared for in the 1930s. But it was not a campaign that Chamberlain was destined to lead. His government had fallen on 10 May, following widespread criticism of its spiritless and ineffectual leadership. On the day that German forces invaded France and the Low Countries, he was succeeded by Winston Churchill. Here was a man whose instincts were flamboyantly bellicose. He relished the conflict in France (Churchill 'likes war' Lloyd George once remarked, not altogether charitably). He was shocked at the defeat of France, and promised French leaders that he would 'fight on for ever and ever and ever'. It was Churchill who on 18 June 1940 memorably defined the coming contest when he told the House of Commons that 'the Battle of France is over. I expect the battle of Britain is about to begin.'[8]

If this speech inspired many, it alienated others. Churchill was not the conductor of a well-drilled orchestra playing in defiant unison. Defeat in Europe in May left British strategy in tatters. Under such dangerous circumstances it is perhaps unsurprising that arguments should surface for a compromise peace with Hitler. The critical turning-point came at the end of May. Prompted by feelers from the Italian ambassador in London, the Foreign Secretary, Lord Halifax, asked the Cabinet to consider the possibility that Britain might have to seek a peace. Halifax was repelled by Churchill's rhetorical style and his *Boy's Own* zest for fighting to the death. After Cabinet on 27 May he complained that the prime minister 'talked the most dreadful rot', and persisted in his effort to base British policy on what he termed 'common sense and not bravado'.[9] A tense meeting on 28 May left Halifax isolated. Churchill had no intention of ending his brief wartime premiership sullied by surrender. The government remained committed to the fight. Though appeasement might have seemed irresistible at such a moment, Chamberlain supported Churchill, a factor overlooked by the many later critics. This was of profound importance, for it brought to his side the bulk of the Conservative Party – many of whom distrusted Churchill as a renegade and a charlatan – together with the Liberal and Labour ranks in Parliament upon whose support Churchill's choice as prime minister had rested. Churchill could now fight Chamberlain's war.

That same day, 28 May, Churchill was asked to approve pre-invasion preparations to ship Britain's national treasures and gold to safe keeping abroad, including the Coronation Chair. He scribbled on the letter: 'I believe we shall make them rue the day they try to invade our island. No such discussion can be permitted.'[10] The public mood was in the main with Churchill. A Home Intelligence report on 28 May revealed a popular conviction that 'we shall pull through in the end'; three days later the people were reportedly more bullish, displaying a 'general calmness' and a 'new feeling of determination'.[11]

But the decision taken in late May to fight on did not still all appetite for peace. A scattered population of defeatists, 'realists' and fellow-travellers endorsed the idea of exploring the prospects for peace with Hitler. They included Basil Liddell Hart, the military strategist; 'RAB' Butler at the Foreign Office; the pacifist socialist Charles Roden Buxton; and an unlikely coupling of British fascists and communists, temporarily bound together by the German–Soviet Pact of August 1939. The peace party's most powerful spokesman was David Lloyd George, Britain's outstanding war leader in 1916–18. His interest in peace stemmed from an inexplicably myopic respect for Hitler (he once described him as 'the George Washington of Germany', and in autumn 1940 numbered Hitler 'among the greatest leaders of men in history'). Around thirty MPs joined in urging Lloyd George to campaign for peace in June 1940. Churchill thought about inviting him to join the Cabinet, but was encouraged by colleagues to think again. Lloyd George did not want to join anyway. He preferred to wait 'until Winston is bust', and waited in vain.[12]

A great deal has been made of the so-called 'peace party', but its historical significance has been vastly inflated. Even Churchill was forced by circumstances to admit the possibility of defeat, though not surrender.

Halifax was never in favour of peace at any price, certainly not at a price that would compromise British sovereignty in any substantial way, and he soon came round to accept that continued belligerency was the only honourable course. The other appeasers were marginalized or ignored. There was still much evidence of the British stiff upper-lip. When the Chiefs of Staff Committee discussed the instructions to be issued to the civil population to prepare for invasion, it was decided that they should be asked to behave 'cheerfully and bravely'. Women, the chiefs of staff declared, were of 'best service' keeping 'their own home running for their own menfolk'.[13] On 30 May Churchill was shown a minute circulated to officials at the Foreign Office by the Permanent Secretary, Sir Alexander Cadogan, asking them not to reveal a glimmer of the appalling news from France: 'We may in our own minds face very unpleasant truths and possibilities, but we have no right to let our friends or acquaintances assume from a chance word or an attitude of depression the anxiety we may feel.' At the foot Churchill added the single word 'Good'.[14]

None the less, the decision to fight on brought weeks of fearfulness and uncertainty. Popular opinion fluctuated with the final crisis in France, but on 17 June, when news came of French surrender, Home Intelligence found only a mood of 'gloomy apprehension', more prominent among 'the middle classes and the women'.[15] There were mutterings picked up by Home Intelligence agents, stationed surreptitiously in bars and cafés, that a Hitler victory might not be such a bad thing. 'Many workers say about Hitler,' ran a report in mid-June, ' "He won't hurt us: it's the bosses he's after: we'll probably be better off when he comes." ' Later reports suggested that the lower middle classes were also vulnerable: 'The whiter the collar, the less the assurance.' But in general, morale reports showed a strengthening resolve across the weeks before the air battles began. While only 50 per cent of respondents in one opinion poll regarded fighting alone with confidence, 75 per cent of those asked wanted war to continue (84 per cent of men, but only 65 per cent of women).[16]

In the prevailing atmosphere there were daily scares about invasion or sabotage or espionage. These fears began right at the top. At the end of May the War Office, responding to intelligence information, began to prepare for a possible German invasion of Ireland. Thanks to the existence of the IRA, described by the Joint Intelligence Committee as 'a very formidable body of revolutionists', whose members were 'violently anti-British and many of them pro-German', Ireland was regarded as prime fifth column territory. The three services were warned to expect 'a German descent upon Eire, in conjunction with subservient members of the IRA'. Though the War Cabinet took the sensible view that southern England remained the key danger-spot, the possibility of diversionary action in Ireland, Scotland or Wales, where it was felt that the Germans could exploit local ethnic grievances along 'Sudeten' lines, remained very much alive.[17]

There were also fears of subversion closer to home. The Air Ministry observed in its 'Plans for Invasion' in June that the 77,000 aliens living in Britain constituted a standing threat and should all be 'deported to the other side of the Atlantic'. The Ministry wanted further evacuation from the cities stopped in order to prevent foreign spies from infiltrating the displaced populations.[18] So anxious did the Ministry of Information become that in July 1940 a 'Silent Column' campaign was launched under the direction of the art historian Kenneth Clark, which aimed at stamping out gossip and rumour. Like most campaigns mounted by the Ministry that year, it proved to be a disaster. Within days there was widespread public hostility to efforts to stifle discussion, and outrage at the few prosecutions. The popular view was that people ought to be able to police themselves. Two weeks after its launch, the 'Silent Column' was abandoned. Official unease persisted, however. As late as January 1941 the Policy Committee of the Information Ministry still bemoaned 'the dangers of the attitude liable to be accepted by the very poor or the very rich that a German victory would not make very much difference'.[19]

Such fears may seem quite unrealistic more than half a century later. Yet they reflect the evident reality that Britain was a country divided by geography and social class, riven by popular prejudices and a complex structure of snobbery. The British public did not speak with one voice; British society adjusted in a variety of ways to the prospect of fighting alone (this is perhaps the most enduring myth, sustained in simple disregard of the vital and substantial support of Canada, South Africa, Australia, New Zealand, India and the colonial empire). If Hitler had won in 1940, it is unrealistic to suppose that Germany would not have confronted in Britain the same unstable mix of active collaborators, silent bystanders and hostile partisans that characterized the populations of all the other states she occupied. Nevertheless, the predominant instinct in the summer of 1940 was to accept, hesitantly perhaps, fearfully certainly, that invasion might happen and that the British people should obstruct it. This was the spirit observed by the American reporter Virginia Cowles, who watched with mounting incredulity the moral revival of the population after the shock of Dunkirk and French defeat: 'For the first time I understood what the maxim meant: "England never knows when she is beaten" ... I was more than impressed. I was flabbergasted. I not only understood the maxim; I understood why Britain never *had* been beaten.'[20]

This was an attitude little appreciated in Berlin. The victory over France transformed the possibilities confronting Hitler, but because victory was so much swifter and more complete than the German side expected, little thought had been given to what might happen next. German leaders believed that Britain had been an unwilling belligerent in September 1939. With France defeated, there no longer appeared any reason for Britain to remain at war. A political settlement seemed likely. Joseph Goebbels, Hitler's Minister of Propaganda, told his staff on 23 June that the Churchill government was doomed: 'A compromise government will be formed. We are very close to the end of the war.'[21] The German army chief of staff, General Franz Halder, recorded in his war diary in July that Hitler favoured 'political and diplomatic procedures' to bring Britain to a settlement. The alternative of crossing the Channel Hitler regarded (rightly) as 'very hazardous'. 'Invasion is to be undertaken,' Halder wrote, 'only if no other way is left to bring terms to

Britain.' In his opinion Britain was in a hopeless position: 'The war is won by us. A reversal in the prospects of success is impossible.'[22]

In the heady days following the defeat of France such confidence was understandable. Yet all the indications showed that the war was far from over as far as the British government were concerned. It has often been assumed that Hitler himself took the initiative in finally proposing invasion as a solution, but it was the German Navy commander-in-chief, Admiral Erich Raeder, who first raised the issue in conferences with Hitler on 21 May and again on 20 June. The navy had been preparing contingency plans since November 1939, and though naval leaders doubted the feasibility of invasion, they were keen to give the navy a role in the aftermath of victory over France, in which they had played a lesser part. However, Raeder's main preference was for a joint air–naval blockade of Britain, which seemed to him to offer prospects for a quick end to the war without an invasion at all. Not wanting to be outbid by the navy, the German army began its own study of the possibility of invasion in late June, in case Hitler should call for plans at short notice.[23]

Exactly when, or why, Hitler decided to take up the navy's suggestion may never be known with certainty, but on 2 July he decided to order the armed forces to undertake exploratory planning, and on 7 July issued a directive to that end for 'the War against England' (German leaders almost never talked of Great Britain, or the wider Empire). This was not yet an operational order, not even a plan. The directive authorized the services to complete the necessary investigations and preparations that would make a plan possible, and they proceeded to do so with mixed enthusiasm. Hitler's decision to explore a military solution probably owed something to the infectious Anglophobia of his Foreign Minister, Joachim von Ribbentrop, a man whose insufferable pomposity repelled even his own colleagues and had made him a laughing stock when he came to London as ambassador in 1936. Ribbentrop was keener than anyone in Hitler's circle to concentrate every effort on defeating Britain. On 1 July German Foreign Office officials were briefed that Germany had no thoughts of peace, but only 'preparation for the destruction of England'.[24]

This could scarcely have been further from the truth. Hitler hoped for a political settlement first and foremost. At a staff meeting shortly before the French capitulation, Hitler announced that as soon as France was finished it was planned 'to send an offer to England, whether England is prepared to end hostilities'.[25] Diplomatic traffic during June and early July suggested that there was room for a political settlement. The German ambassador in Moscow, Friedrich von der Schulenburg, reported on 5 July a conversation between the Swedish ambassador and Sir Stafford Cripps, recently appointed to the British embassy. Cripps, with a disarming lack of that discretion so much in demand at home, claimed that the democracies 'were hopelessly behind the authoritarian states, that the attack on the island [Britain] will probably succeed'. A British diplomat in Bern openly discussed the need for peace talks, and dismissed Churchill as a dilettante and a drunk. The heavily staffed German embassy in Dublin engaged in feverish attempts to find out what was happening in London, but could only forward to Berlin the very dubious intelligence that the lower and middle classes wanted peace, while the upper classes wanted war.[26]

Hitler was in no rush to settle with Britain. In the absence of any clear signals from London, he decided to seize the initiative by announcing publicly that the door to a peaceful settlement was not closed if the British were prepared to ask for one. Ribbentrop was told on 6 July to draft a speech for Hitler to deliver to the Reichstag on 19 July. The draft was not what he wanted, and Hitler rewrote the speech himself. In the interim his attitude to Britain began to harden. On 7 July, the day he directed the armed forces to explore the possibility of invasion, he told the Italian Foreign Minister, Count Galeazzo Ciano, that he was now more inclined 'to unleash a storm of wrath and steel upon the British'.[27] A week later he instructed the armed forces to prepare an invasion to take place at any time after 15 August. On 16 July he finally published War Directive 16 for 'Operation Sealion', a surprise landing somewhere on the British coastline between Ramsgate and the Isle of Wight, to take place if other kinds of political and military pressure failed. Invasion was a last resort; it was only possible, the directive warned, if air superiority could be established over southern England and a safe area of sea secured for the crossing.[28]

Three days later Hitler delivered his peace offer. Goebbels' Propaganda Ministry made elaborate technical preparations to have the speech broadcast worldwide. The deputies assembled in the Kroll Opera House, home to the German parliament since the fire-raising of the Reichstag building in February 1933. Overhead, German fighter aircraft flew on patrol to prevent a sudden bomb attack. Hitler spoke without the usual wild oratory, and received none of the usual bays of approval and stamping of feet. Above him sat row upon row of bemedalled soldiers. In the chair sat Hermann Goering, commander-in-chief of the German Air Force and Reichstag president, writing out his vote of thanks as Hitler talked. Count Ciano sat with an Italian text of the speech, and jumped up to salute in all the wrong places. The peace offer constituted no more than a fraction of what was in effect a celebration of German victory. Its wording was haughty and condescending. Hitler blamed the war on the Jews, Freemasons and armament kings who kept the Allied peoples in thrall; he had no desire to destroy the British Empire, but would bring it down in ruins if war went on; he appealed to British common sense to end the war, but he appealed 'as a conqueror'.[29]

It was a clever speech. The continuation of the war was placed entirely at the British door; Hitler basked in the unaccustomed role of the magnanimous victor. It was sincerely meant, if only in the sense that German leaders did want Britain to sue for peace on their terms. Hitler made no secret of his disappointment when the British rejected his offer. German officials and soldiers sat listening to the British reaction on the BBC German service later on the evening of 19 July. William Shirer, a young American newsman, sat with them and listened to their howls of disbelief: ' "Can you understand those British fools? To turn down peace now? They're crazy." '[30] In London Hitler's speech caused scarcely a ripple. Lord

Halifax gave a formal rejection over the radio on the evening of 22 July, which was widely criticized in Britain not only for the lame delivery, but for the seventeen references to God. When the War Cabinet next assembled, the peace offer was not even discussed. The same day, 23 July, at the daily press conference in Berlin, reporters were told by an angry official: 'Gentlemen, there will be war.'[31]

The British rejection needs little explanation. The decision to continue the fight against Germany had already been made some weeks before. Though it is sometimes argued that Britain would have lost less by reaching a compromise in 1940, rejection was, under the circumstances, an entirely rational decision. Nothing in Hitler's record could give any serious grounds for the British to expect Hitler to honour any pledges entered into. The treatment of the other conquered peoples was evident to the whole world; even unconquered, Britain was expected by the German side to make very substantial concessions and to pay extensive reparation. Only days after the rejection of Hitler's offer, harsh terms were finally revealed for the territorial dismemberment of defeated France. At the same time a 'New Order' for the European economy was announced, with a privileged Germany at its core. British interests were, under such circumstances, fundamentally incompatible with German hegemony across Europe.

It is more difficult to gauge German intentions. Was Hitler serious about the war against Britain? The British public was never in any doubt in 1940 that Hitler wanted to invade if he could. The German records show less certainty. Three conferences on 21, 25 and 31 July reveal strong doubts not about the desirability, but over the operational feasibility of invasion. The third of these meetings, called on 31 July between Hitler and his military chiefs, also supplies the first evidence that Hitler was now thinking of a large-scale campaign against the Soviet Union in 1941. This plan, like Operation Sealion, did not originate with Hitler. The German army undertook contingency planning at the beginning of July for a brief operation against the Red Army with the limited objective of securing German predominance throughout eastern Europe, and keeping the Soviet Union at arm's length. During June 1940 the Soviet Union had taken advantage of Germany's war in the west to absorb the Baltic States and the Romanian province of Bessarabia. This growing threat took Hitler beyond the idea of a mere limited strike; on 31 July he instead suggested a massive campaign to annihilate the Soviet system in one blow. This campaign would secure German hegemony in the east and access to the vast food and material resources of western

Asia. Preparatory work was authorized, though a final directive for what became known as 'Operation Barbarossa' was not issued until 18 December.[32]

Such evidence has been used to suggest that the war in the west was continued only to lull Soviet suspicions, and that invasion was never seriously contemplated. This is to distort the reality. The campaigns against Britain and the Soviet Union were not alternatives. Hitler was genuinely uncertain about how to bring about either a political or military settlement with Britain, and kept several strings to his bow. He was willing to seize opportunities as they arose. He hoped that blockade and air attack might so reduce British resolve and undermine the capacity to fight that invasion would be little more than a mopping-up operation. The preparations made for the campaign were far too extensive for a mere feint. If the campaign did not work, and there was no certainty that it would, an assault on the Soviet Union, he told his commanders, would remove Britain's last hope of continuing the war, even with American assistance. Either way, the object was sooner or later to destroy British power. If the RAF could be defeated, it might be sooner.

# TWO THE ADVERSARIES

The situation as it presents itself for our Air Force for the decisive struggle against Britain is as favourable as it can be . . . What will happen when the German Air Force employs its whole strength against England? The game looks bad for England and her geographical and military isolation. We can face with confidence the great decision to come!

**General Quade, former commandant,**
**Luftwaffe Staff College, July 1940**[1]

The military confrontation in the autumn of 1940 became a test of strength between two rival air forces. The other services waited on the outcome. Armies on both sides of the Channel trained for the coming battle. Navies waited to contest the narrow seas across which German soldiers would have to be conveyed in makeshift transports and hastily converted barges. But none of this mattered as long as the German Air Force had not yet won mastery of the air over southern Britain. For Hitler this was the essential precondition for invasion. 'If the effect of the air attacks,' he told Admiral Raeder at the end of July, 'is such that the enemy air force, harbours, and naval forces, etc., are heavily damaged, operation "Sea Lion" will be carried out in 1940.' If Germany's air force could not achieve what would now be called the 'degrading' of British air and naval forces, Hitler proposed postponing invasion until May 1941.[2]

The two air forces that fought what later came to be called the Battle of Britain were led and organized in very different ways. The contrast was personified at the very top, in the choice of air minister. This was a difference typical of the gulf that separated a populist, authoritarian dictatorship from a parliamentary democracy dominated by established elites. Germany's air minister was the flamboyant National Socialist Hermann Goering, a decorated First World War fighter pilot with the famous Richthofen Squadron. He was an 'old fighter' of the Party, who had risen to become one of the principal political playmakers of the Third Reich. He became minister in 1933, and in 1935 also became the German Air Force commander-in-chief, combining both administrative and military responsibilities. Thanks to his considerable political weight, the air force was built almost from the ground up in only six years. He was a vain and ruthless man, a crude popular orator, a corrupt and ambitious lieutenant whose power expanded during the 1930s in step with Germany's massive remilitarization. The popular image of a baroque, drug-dependent sybarite is largely caricature. As a commander he lacked judgement, but he did not lack energy or interest. From early August 1940 Goering assumed direct command of the air war against Britain.

Britain's air minister was Sir Archibald Sinclair. He had been second-in-command of the battalion that Churchill briefly led on the Western Front in 1915–16. After the war he went on to a career as a Liberal Member of Parliament, and by 1940 was leader of the Liberal fraction in the Commons. He had no experience of air power (though his parliamentary under-secretary had flown in the Royal Flying Corps during the First World War). Churchill appointed him to his post on the day he became prime minister, which left him with less than three months in office before the onset of the battle. Sinclair was straight out of that rich British tradition of the gifted amateur. As a result he was not regarded as a particularly good minister, though by all accounts a good parliamentary speaker, and a committed defender of the force he represented. His virtues, according to Sir Maurice Dean, who worked with Sinclair throughout the war, were those of the British genteel establishment: 'thoroughly competent, completely devoted and highly respected . . . a great gentleman'.[3] Sinclair epitomized that British elite of dignified public servants so much despised and ridiculed in German propaganda. Goering, on the other hand, was everything Sinclair was not.

Sinclair, unlike his opposite number, made no pretence at leading the Royal Air Force. The British system did not include a commander-in-chief for each defence service. It was a system run by committees. The military side of the British air effort was placed under the Air Staff, whose leader sat on the Chiefs of Staff Committee, where all major issues of strategy and operations were decided. In August 1940 this position was held by Air Chief Marshal Sir Cyril Newall, a career airman nearing the end of his tenure. He was not regarded as an inspirational leader. Like Sinclair's, Newall's is not a name that has entered the Battle of Britain pantheon. He was none the less one of the key architects of RAF expansion in the critical years between 1937 and 1940, and a keen defender of air force interests. The British system required effective committee men and military managers; Newall did not command the battle, but he made it possible to fight.

It was the commander-in-chief of Fighter Command, Air Chief Marshal Sir Hugh Dowding, who gave battle to Goering. In 1940 he was already fifty-nine years old and at the end of his career. The son of a Devon schoolmaster, he joined the army in 1899 and served in India and the Far East. A keen skier and polo-player, he taught himself to fly and became a reserve officer in the fledgling Royal Flying Corps in 1914. In the First World War he flew regularly in combat, though already a senior officer in his mid-thirties. In 1916 he was posted to Training Command, and his front-line assignment given to Newall, a former officer in the Gurkhas and the future chief of staff. Dowding became a career air officer in the post-war RAF and when the service was reorganized into separate commands in 1936, he was appointed to lead Fighter Command. Unlike the German system of air fleets, each of which was composed of a mixed force of fighters, bombers, dive-bombers, etc., the RAF was organized functionally, with separate commands for fighters, bombers, coastal aircraft, reserves, training and, later, maintenance. The new system was designed to improve the efficiency and fighting power of the air service; in Fighter Command it produced an organization ideal for the unified defence of the British Isles.

Dowding devoted himself to the task of creating that defensive shield, and in the process was often at logger-heads with the Air Ministry and the Air Staff. His merited reputation as a prickly and independent-minded com-mander is often used to explain the decision to retire him in June 1939, but he had simply come to the end of his term of appointment. When his designated successor suffered an air accident, the Air Ministry decided, given the tense international situation, to keep Dowding on until March 1940. At the last moment, on 30 March, Newall wrote to him asking him to retain his office until 14 July. On the very brink of the air battle, Dowding still expected to retire. On 5 July, however, with Churchill's backing, Newall asked Dowding for the third time to remain in office a little longer, until 31 October. Dowding huffily consented, but he fought the Battle of Britain with retirement hanging over his head.[4]

The Command that Dowding led in July 1940 was composed of four operational groups. The front line in south-east England was held by 11 Group, commanded by the New Zealand airman Air Vice-Marshal Keith Park, who had been Dowding's deputy staff officer in the 1930s. North of London was 12 Group under Air Vice-Marshal Trafford Leigh-Mallory. The north of England and Scotland were defended by 13 Group, and the west and south-west by 10 Group, which comprised only a handful of squadrons. On 19 June, at the end of the campaign in France, Fighter Command had only 768 fighters in operational squadrons, and of these only 520 were fit for operations. By 9 August, shortly before the launch of the full German air offensive, the situation had improved significantly. There were now 1,032 aircraft at operational bases, of which 715 were immediately ready for operations. There were a further 424 aircraft in storage units, ready for use the next day.[5] These figures remained more or less constant throughout the coming battle.

One of the most enduring myths of the Battle of Britain is the idea of the few against the many. The official battle narrative produced by the Air Ministry talked of the unequalled achievement of 'a force so small, facing one so large'.[6] Yet on 10 August 1940, the German single-engined fighter forces assigned to the battle over Britain had an operational establishment of 1,011, slightly fewer than Fighter Command. They enjoyed a marginally better serviceability record, with 805 fighters immediately ready for operations. It is, of course, true that Fighter Command was spread across Britain, while the German fighter force concentrated attacks on the south. It is true, too, that Fighter Command also faced enemy bombers, dive-bombers and heavy twin-engined fighters deployed in the battle, but apart from the heavy fighters, which were outmatched in combat, the bombers and dive-bombers were not a major threat to fighter aircraft, whose job it was to shoot them down while trying to avoid enemy fighters themselves. Air superiority for the German side meant defeating the enemy fighter force, as it did later for the Anglo-American air forces in their bombing offensive over Germany. During the course of the battle, Fighter Command maintained its numbers despite high losses;

but by 7 September the German Air Force was reduced to 533 serviceable single-engined fighters. On 1 October the number fell temporarily to 275. Early in the battle there was a rough parity in fighter numbers; in the last weeks Fighter Command had the edge.

The key to this success was aircraft production. During 1940 the numbers of fighter aircraft initially planned for production were substantially exceeded. The Harrogate Programme published in January 1940 designated the output of 3,602 fighters during 1940. Actual production reached 4,283 over the year, and rose very substantially from June onwards throughout the months of the air conflict. In May Churchill appointed his old friend Lord Beaverbrook, the owner of *Express* newspapers, as Minister of Aircraft Production in the hope that his energy and experience might speed up aircraft deliveries for the coming battle. Though he harried and bullied the manufacturers, it was not his urgent activity alone that produced the finished aircraft. The large-scale output of aircraft was possible only after a considerable period of gestation and could not be conjured out of thin air. The expansion of output in the summer of 1940 was the fruit of earlier preparation under Newall's stewardship.

Nevertheless, real anxieties existed about the supply of aircraft. Throughout the battle, equipment had to be sent overseas to meet the demands of the war against Italy in North Africa. It is easy to forget that the RAF was forced to fight on two fronts in the summer of 1940, following Italy's declaration of war on 10 June. Between July and October 161 fighters were sent to the Middle East, including 72 Hurricanes.[7] It was hoped that this outflow might be compensated by a swelling stream of aircraft from North America, where Britain placed orders for 14,000 aeroplanes. The results were disappointing. During the period between July and the end of October some 509 aircraft were imported, half of them from late September when the air battle was nearly over. This figure included only 29 Hurricanes produced under licence in Canada, and a mixture of trainer and light bomber aircraft; there were no other fighters for the battle.[8] In May, the fiercely anti-communist Lord Beaverbrook suggested the unusual step of buying fighters from the Soviet Union. Cripps, the British ambassador in Moscow, thought the prospects 'improbable'. The Air Staff, with little enthusiasm, agreed that the I 16 fighter might be 'usable', at least in the Middle East theatre. The Chinese ambassador in London volunteered the services of his country as a go-between in the trade, but when Cripps finally approached the Soviet side in June, he was told to wait until Anglo-Soviet trade was on a sounder footing.[9]

Britain was forced to fight with what she could produce herself in 1940. The aircraft available for the battle were among the very best fighter aircraft in the world. There is no myth surrounding the performance of the Hawker Hurricane and the Vickers Supermarine Spitfire, which between them formed the backbone of Fighter Command. The other aircraft available, the Bristol Blenheim twin-engined fighter and the Boulton-Paul Defiant, lacked the performance necessary to compete with German aircraft by day and were converted early in the battle to a night-fighter role. There were never more than a few squadrons throughout the battle, two of Defiants and six of Blenheims. Bristol Beaufighters began to appear late in the battle as night-fighters.

The great bulk of Fighter Command was composed of Hurricanes. The almost complete identification of the Spitfire with the Battle of Britain has come to obscure the true balance of power between the two models. Spitfires only became available in quantity in the late spring of 1940. Spitfire production lagged substantially behind Hurricane output until early 1941. (See Table 1 p. 159.) Hurricanes provided 65 per cent of the combined output of the two models, Spitfires 35 per cent. In early August, Hurricanes supplied 55 per cent of operational fighter aircraft, Spitfires only 31 per cent, and 11 Group throughout the battle had twice as many Hurricane squadrons as Spitfire.[10] The most telling statistic is the loss ratio. From early May to the end of October 1940, Spitfires accounted for almost 40 per cent of combined losses, while constituting only one-third of the force. Spitfires were shot down faster than Hurricanes.[11]

Both aircraft were at the cutting edge of fighter technology. The Spitfire Mark IA carried an armament of eight .303 machine-guns, the Mark IB (used experimentally in August 1940) had four .303 machine-guns and two 20 mm cannon. The Mark II, which began to arrive in June 1940, had a higher rate of climb and higher service ceiling, but was slightly slower – 354 mph against 362 mph at 18,000 feet. The Hurricane was a slower aircraft, but sturdier. The Hurricane Mark I had armament of eight .303 machine-guns, and had a maximum speed of 325 mph, and an average of 305 mph. The Mark IIA had a maximum speed of 342 mph, and was delivered in small numbers from August 1940. Both marks had a ceiling of 34–35,000 feet.

There was room for improvement on both designs. The Hurricane had a number of drawbacks, but the most serious was the failure to supply a self-sealing fuel tank in the fuselage. The tank, positioned close to the pilot, was easily ignited and was the cause of serious burns for any pilots lucky enough to survive the experience. The pilot canopy was also difficult to dislodge before baling out, and was later modified. Dowding urged Hawker from early in 1940 to seal the fuselage tanks with 'Linatex', but not until the battle was the modification slowly carried out. During the battle both Spitfires and Hurricanes had their less-effective two-pitch propellors replaced with constant-speed propellors, which improved general handling qualities and gave them an extra 7,000 feet of ceiling. A more serious problem was the supply of effective armament. Although the eight-gun fighter was regarded as an advance on German models, the .303 armament could not penetrate the armour installed in German fighters and bombers. Mixed armament was supplied for the eight guns in the hope that a mixture of armour-piercing and incendiary bullets would hit something vulnerable. But in his despatch on the battle, Dowding concluded that with better armament higher casualties could have been inflicted on the enemy.[12]

The supply of trained fighter pilots promised to be a much more damaging constraint on Fighter Command operations than the supply of aircraft. Yet this deficiency can be wildly exaggerated. The number of fighter pilots available for operations increased by one-third between June and August 1940. The personnel records show an almost constant supply of around 1,400 pilots during the crucial weeks of the battle, and over 1,500 in the second half of September. The shortfall of pilots was seldom above 10 per cent of the force. The German single-seater fighter force, on the other hand, had between 1,100 and 1,200 pilots, with around 800–900 available for operations, a deficiency of up to one-third. The German fighter force was able to cope with this shortage only because it enjoyed a lower rate of loss than Fighter Command.[13] If Fighter Command were the 'few', German fighter pilots were fewer.

Little of this was appreciated at the time on the British side. Air Intelligence estimated that the German Air Force had around 16,000 pilots in the spring of 1940, with at least 7,300 in operational units.[14] There was a flurry of activity to try to raise pilot output to match these numbers. The training system was overhauled in the summer of 1940 with the addition of three operational training units capable of supplying 115 pilots instead of 39 every two weeks. This did not satisfy Churchill, who badgered the Air Ministry all summer with unhelpful suggestions for getting men into the cockpit. When he discovered that 1,600 qualified pilots were assigned to staff duties and a further 2,000 to training, he demanded an urgent inquiry, despite Sinclair's assurance that most of the men were over-age or under-trained. More was expected of the many foreign airmen who made their way to Britain during 1940. By June they included some 1,500 Poles, who were undergoing training near Blackpool. Churchill was determined 'to make the most of the Poles', and in early July the War Cabinet authorized the creation of two all-Polish squadrons for Fighter Command.[15] By August there was also a Canadian and a Czech squadron, but the rest of the Command had its share of American, Irish, Commonwealth and European volunteers. Two of the four Group commanders were non-British: Park was a New Zealander and Brand, commander of 10 Group, was South African.

Where there were obvious deficiencies was in the supply of non-combat personnel needed to make the whole Command organization work efficiently. There were shortages of manpower of all kinds at the air stations: fitters (grades I and II), armourers, instrument mechanics, maintenance and construction workers. There were shortages of signals personnel, which was a real drawback for a force that relied on communication. It was discovered in the summer that because of losses in France there was a dangerous shortage of tanker lorries for refuelling aircraft. Churchill's response to this news was simply to exhort the ground crews to work faster: 'the turn-around of aircraft in units should be a drill comparable with the Navy's gun drill at Olympia'.[16]

Technical problems like these may seem trivial when set against the sombre prospect of invasion, but they were the necessary components of a complex system of 'command and control' which gave Fighter Command a real striking power and operational flexibility. The heart of the system lay at Command headquarters at Bentley Priory in Stanmore, on the outskirts of London. It was here, in the Filter Room, that information on incoming aircraft was relayed by landline from all the radar stations around the coast. The plots were laid out on a large map table, and once the aircraft track was clearly established, this information was relayed in turn to the Group Headquarters and the individual Sector Stations (airfields). Additional intelligence was supplied by the Observer Corps whose members plotted enemy aircraft visually once they had crossed the coast. This information went first to an Observer Corps Centre, and then straight to Sector Stations and Group Headquarters. Group commanders then had to decide which of their sectors to activate, while Sector Station commanders were responsible for deciding which of their squadrons should fly on a particular operation. Once airborne, aircraft were controlled by Radio-Telephony Direction-Finding

(R/T-D/F). The whole process was supposed to take minutes only. Without speed and clear instructions the system was pointless.[17]

The entire structure of communication was dependent on early warning and continuous observation. The heart of the system was the Radio Direction Finding (RDF) apparatus, better known as radar. The technology was first developed in 1935 when it was demonstrated that aircraft reflected back to ground short-wave radio pulses, which could be captured on a cathode ray tube. By 1939 there were 21 so-called Chain Home radar stations circling Britain's coastline, theoretically capable of detecting the height and range of approaching aircraft up to 200 miles distant. Average range was only 80 miles, but adequate for the German air threat across the Channel. The radar stations could not detect aircraft flying below 1,000 feet, and a second system of Chain Home Low stations was established after the outbreak of war to detect low-flying aircraft and coastal shipping. These stations had a range of only 30 miles and could not predict height, though that mattered less at such low altitudes.

Radar could not yet work inland. It had to be supplemented by the Observer Corps, formally founded in 1929, and commanded in 1940 by Air Commodore A. D. Warrington-Morris. It was staffed by volunteers across the country who largely trained themselves in aircraft recognition and methods of height estimation. On the outbreak of war there were 30,000 observers and 1,000 observation posts, each armed with a grid map, a height estimator, telephone, coloured map markers and the means to make tea. Posts were manned continuously; the system worked well in fine weather, but was defeated by low cloud cover and rain. Height estimation was difficult and often inaccurate. Group headquarters found that numerous Observer Corps plots cluttered up the map tables with a surfeit of less reliable information.[18]

Radar, too, was by no means infallible. Height readings could be thousands of feet out; the time-lag was at times too long between sighting enemy aircraft and scrambling fighters to meet them (it took a minimum of four minutes for the squadrons to receive radar warning, but only six minutes for enemy aircraft to cross the Channel); radar equipment was continuously upgraded, which left some stations inoperable for brief periods while new technology was installed. By the time of the battle, secret intelligence was being supplied from decrypts of German Air Force 'Enigma' traffic, but although this was useful in building up a clearer picture of the German order of battle, it was less useful in giving information quickly enough on the scale and destination of major raids. This was not the case with low-level radio interception, whose role has generally been neglected. The RAF wireless interception station at Cheadle took advantage of the slack radio discipline displayed by German aircrew to supply a regular diet of accurate reports on range, destination and origin of aircraft which was relayed directly to Command headquarters as well as Group and Sector commanders. The net effect of all these different sources of intelligence was to create a web of information that gave Fighter Command an essential counter to the element of surprise enjoyed by an enemy who could pick and choose when and where to attack.[19]

Fighter defence was supplemented by a network of anti-aircraft guns and barrage balloons. Anti-Aircraft Command was established only in April 1939. Headed by Lieutenant-General Sir Frederick Pile, it was integrated with Fighter Command to provide a unitary defence network. A crash production programme for anti-aircraft artillery was pushed through, but could not make up for severe deficiencies. By June 1940 there were 1,204 heavy and 581 light anti-aircraft guns to cover the entire country, far short of the planned 2,232 heavy and 1,860 light guns. The batteries were activated, like the fighter stations, from Fighter Command headquarters. The country was divided into 130 warning districts, based on the layout of the national telephone system. Three telephone operators at headquarters kept in continuous contact with trunk-exchanges in London, Liverpool and Glasgow. When enemy aircraft were 20 miles distant, a 'yellow' warning was sent to the endangered districts to place emergency services on alert. Five minutes later a 'red' alert would follow and air-raid sirens would start up, followed shortly by the anti-aircraft barrage. 'Green' indicated that the aircraft had passed and signalled the all-clear. It was a system that worked almost too well. During the summer of 1940 whole areas of the country were sent scurrying into air-raid shelters at the distant approach of a handful of aircraft. The disruption to normal work-time brought the government to the point of abandoning air-raid warning altogether. In June 1940 the Minister of Information, Duff Cooper, suggested that people should accustom themselves 'to receiving no warnings when only a few aircraft were in the neighbourhood, even if these aircraft dropped bombs', but the Cabinet sensibly opted to retain some element of warning.[20]

The air defence system was set up to counter an enemy bombing offensive and to ameliorate its effects on the bombed population. In the summer of 1940 it had to be adjusted to the threat of invasion. The two operations were by no means the same. Invasion presented Fighter

Command with a range of new responsibilities, including close collaboration with Bomber Command, whose aircraft had to be protected as they pounded the invasion beaches. Provisional plans were considered as early as October 1939 when it was agreed to supply the army with two squadrons of Blenheims and one army co-operation squadron to repel an invasion force. The assumption underlying this feeble gesture was that no invasion could be attempted until Fighter Command had been neutralized, and that the real battle would be fought in the skies over southern England long before invasion could be undertaken.[21]

By the summer of 1940 invasion was a much more realistic threat. Fighter Command was instructed by the commander-in-chief of Home Forces, General Sir Alan Brooke, to prevent the German Air Force from achieving air superiority and to protect airfields and other vital military targets. At the same time fighters were expected to attack, in order of priority, enemy transport aircraft bringing in men and supplies, enemy dive-bombers, high-flying reconnaissance aircraft and enemy fighters attacking RAF bombers over the invasion area. This dizzy list was enlarged in late summer by additional requirements to protect naval vessels and bases and to attack enemy barges and sea transports with cannon-armed fighters. Bomber Command, meanwhile, was asked to attack ports of embarkation by night. During invasion, bombers were needed immediately over the invasion beaches, where it was hoped invasion could be nipped in the bud in no more than forty-eight hours of 'utmost physical and mental effort'.[22]

Much thought was given to subterfuge. In the October directive it had been assumed that Germany might try to seize airfields using small units of tough airborne troops.[23] German success in capturing the fortress of Liège in May 1940 gave real substance to the fear, and priority was given to strengthening airfield defence. The results were often lamentable. Two separate inspections were undertaken by army commanders. They found some anti-aircraft guns placed on the roofs of vulnerable buildings, others scarcely concealed, and many incapable of either seeing or engaging low-flying aircraft. Many stations had neither barbed wire nor pill-boxes. It had been decided that RAF ground personnel should not be armed, so that airfields had to rely on local army units, which would be expected to arrive only after a delay of one to two hours, and in force in only four hours. In August, RAF airfield staff were given arms again, but were not yet properly trained in their use.[24] Reports showed that when enemy aircraft occasionally landed on British airfields, they were able to take off again unmolested.

There were also fears that German forces would use poison gas to achieve swift mastery of key front-line airfields. To this threat the only answer was deemed to be retaliation in kind. The Air Ministry sent stores of gas bombs (chiefly mustard gas) to airfields, where they were prepared ready for use at three hours' notice. The Air Staff preferred the idea of using gas against soldiers on the invasion beaches to be sure of containing the threat at once, but Churchill and the chiefs of staff instructed the Air Ministry in late September to plan for gas attacks on the German civilian population in case gas was used by the Germans in the early stages of invasion.[25] Gas attacks were also considered in the special case of a German surprise attack on Ireland, a fantasy that still lived on in Whitehall circles throughout the summer and autumn of 1940. In late June the Air Staff directed the small air force stationed in Northern Ireland to prepare for an attack on German troops 'and I.R.A. irregulars co-operating with them'. Bomber aircraft were to fly from the mainland bringing either gas or high-explosive bombs. All air crew were asked to exercise 'particular discretion' when attacking targets south of the border 'which may cause loss of life to Irish civilians'.[26] This prospect must have seemed a peculiarly daunting one for the force of 12 fighters and 20 light bombers available in Northern Ireland to repel the hitherto unstoppable *Wehrmacht*.

In the end, none of these fears materialized, neither the gas and airborne assault, nor the invasion of Ireland. German military leaders recognized that the preliminary to any land operation was the elimination of the enemy air force, and made their plans accordingly. Victory over France transformed the prospects for a successful air campaign for it allowed the German Air Force to fly from any point on the European coastline from Norway to Brittany. The critical factor for the German side was the short range of the Messerschmitt Me 109 single-engined fighter. Flying from Germany, it would have had hardly any time for combat over southern England; even flying from bases in northern France, the Me 109 could only reach as far as London. When engaged in heavy combat, which used up fuel more rapidly, London was difficult to reach. Some efforts were made to extend fighter range. A disposable drop fuel tank made of moulded plywood was developed before the war, but it was prone to leak and easy to ignite, and was not used. In the summer of 1940 experiments were conducted in towing fighter aircraft for the first part of their flight, but this tactic was also abandoned.[27] Prior to invasion, the German Air Force could only contest air superiority across an arc stretched over Kent, Sussex and Surrey.

The air forces that faced Fighter Command were never-theless stretched out around the northern European lit-toral. Air Fleet 5 was stationed in Norway, and could only attack with long-range aircraft. Preliminary skirmishes by day in August showed that these aircraft would take unacceptably high losses both from enemy action and the long over-sea flight, and Air Fleet 5 took no further part in the battle. The territory covered by Air Fleet 2 stretched from northern Germany, through Belgium and the Netherlands as far as Le Havre in occupied France. Fighter squadrons were clustered in and around the Pas de Calais, close to their targets. To the west lay Air Fleet 3, which had a much larger complement of bombers and dive-bombers for the attack on coastal areas and naval targets.

Air Fleets 2 and 3 were led by two middle-aged Bav-arians, the cream of the new generation of air force commanders appointed in 1935 when the German Air Force was refounded. Air Fleet 2 was led by Field Marshal Albert Kesselring, recently promoted for his contribution to the defeat of France. He is best remembered for his stubborn and occasionally brutal defence of northern Italy against Anglo-American armies later in the war, when he once again reverted to his original career as an army officer. Though lacking air experience, he proved an able organizer, with a genuine authority. His geniality made him a popular leader. Kesselring's fellow commander in charge of Air Fleet 3 was Field Marshal Hugo Sperrle, who led the notorious German Condor Legion during the Spanish Civil War. He, too, was a career army officer, with limited flying experience from the First World War. Sperrle, like Kesselring, was energetic and popular, his corpulence a match for that of his plump commander-in-chief. Though neither had the long air force experience of Newall or Dowding, they brought with them all the qualities of organizational and operational understanding that set the German army apart in the early years of the war.

The task the two commanders faced in the summer of 1940 was one poorly anticipated in the 1930s. The German Air Force had to adjust in short measure from the role of close army support to a campaign of independent air operations against a well-armed air enemy. This change brought a host of practical problems. A whole network of air bases had to be established across northern France. Some existing French air stations could be used, but even these needed to be supplied with stocks of food, oil and spare parts to function effectively. The repair organization, vital for maintaining high levels of serviceability, was more difficult to improvise locally, and many damaged aircraft had to make their way by road and rail back to the Reich for repairs. In order to cope with the new conditions, German fighter forces were gathered into separate operational commands, rather on the lines of the British Group. However, they lacked two significant advantages enjoyed by the RAF: they had no way of tracking where the enemy was, and there was no way of controlling the whole fighter force from the ground once it was airborne.[28]

The German Air Force also operated throughout the coming battle with low levels of reserves. This was largely a consequence of the poor performance of German aircraft production. Even though Hitler granted special priority in June to the air and naval armaments needed to subdue Britain, the supply of aircraft remained sluggish throughout 1940. Pre-war planning had anticipated a doubling of aircraft production in the first year of war to reach more than 20,000, but these targets were regularly scaled down during 1939 to match factory output. Plan 15, in September 1939, and Plan 16, drawn up only two months later, both reduced planned production in 1940 to little more than 11,000. A new plan was drafted in July 1940, but it offered even lower output for the second half of the year. Some effort was made to give fighter production greater priority, but during 1940 only 1,870 single-engined fighters were produced against a planned output of 2,412.[29] This was less than half the British figure. During the summer and autumn of 1940, output of the Me 109 reached 164 in June, 220 in July, 173 in August and 218 in September, a grand total of 775 against the 1,900 fighters produced in Britain.[30]

There were many causes for the deficiency but complacency was not one of them. Goering pressured and bullied the aircraft industry every bit as much as Beaverbrook. Nor were the resources lacking. The German aviation industry had access to the most advanced aeronautical technology in the world and enjoyed larger resources of machinery, raw materials and manpower than the British. The answer must be sought elsewhere. The leading culprit was the head of air force procurement, Colonel Ernst Udet. If ever there was a square peg in a round hole, it was Udet. A former First World War fighter ace, he became a well-known stuntman and film-star in the 1920s, and was a noted cartoonist. He gravitated to Goering's social circle, and was chosen out of the blue to head the air force technical office in 1936, partly because of his popular reputation, partly because Goering wanted a subordinate who posed no threat to his authority. Udet was a ladies' man and *bon viveur*, a daring test pilot and man of action, but he was also a political lightweight who found himself utterly out of his depth in a senior bureaucratic post in which long experience and wide technical knowledge were irreplaceable assets. He was manipulated and misled by the businessmen and officials who surrounded him. Later, in 1941, in desperation at his impossible position, he committed suicide, scrawling on the wall of his apartment before he died that Goering had betrayed him to 'Jews' in the Air Ministry.[31] His place was taken too late by Field Marshal Erhard Milch, state secretary in the Air Ministry and a former director of Lufthansa, who had been sidelined by Goering in the late 1930s because he threatened to be too competent.

The German Air Force was still a formidable enemy in 1940. It was armed with some of the best combat aircraft then available. The high standard of production and the technical complexity of German aircraft provide at least part of the explanation why Udet found it so difficult to raise the production threshold quickly. In the Messerschmitt Me 109 (also known as the Bf (Bayerische Flugzeugwerke) 109) Germany possessed arguably the world's best all-round fighter aircraft. The bulk of the force that fought in the battle bore the suffixes E-1 and E-3, variants with improved engine performance introduced during the course of 1939 and 1940. The Me 109E-1 had a top speed of 334 mph at 19,000 feet, and a ceiling of 34,000 feet. It was armed with two 20 mm cannon and two

7.9 mm machine-guns. The cannon provided a less rapid rate of fire than British fighter weapons, but the explosive shells were more effective. In the summer, armour was added to give the pilot enhanced protection. The Me 109E could be out-turned by both the Hurricane and the Spitfire (though whether this was due to the fact that British aircraft used higher-octane aviation fuel remains open to debate); at heights above 20,000 feet, however, the performance gap between the two sides widened considerably in the Messerschmitt's favour. Because German engines were fitted with a two-stage supercharger, the Me 109 could fight much more robustly at high altitude than it could at the lower levels flown by German bombers. If the Battle of Britain had been fought at 30,000 feet, the RAF would have lost it.[32]

The other German aircraft used extensively in the battle were less effective. The second fighter employed was the Messerschmitt Me 110C/110D twin-engined heavy fighter. It could fly further than the Me 109, and had a comparable speed of 336 mph at 19,000 feet, but it proved much less manoeuvrable than the smaller fighters, and its range was much less than expected under combat conditions. The Me 110's purpose was to lure enemy fighters into battle, allowing the bombers that followed them to fly on to their targets unmolested. In the event the Me 110 had itself to be protected by the Me 109 to prevent insupport-able losses. When the Me 110 flew beyond single-seater fighter range, it proved a sitting duck. The British thought that the German Air Force flew a third fighter, the Heinkel He 113, but it proved to be a figment of the imagination. The only aircraft with this designation was a twin-seat dive-bomber developed in 1936, but the model was renumbered the He 118 by its designer because Heinkel feared pilot superstition. The aircraft remained jinxed none the less; when Udet test-flew it himself in June 1936, it broke up in mid-air and he narrowly escaped with his life. The He 118 never saw service. Its mistaken identification in the battle has been attributed to German misinformation.

German bomber aircraft were generally no match for the RAF. The Junkers Ju 87B dive-bomber suffered the same fate as the Me 110. Much slower than the heavy fighter, it was highly vulnerable during bomb attack and was withdrawn early in the battle. The standard twin-engined bombers, the Heinkel 111 and Dornier 17, were early designs and faced obsolescence by 1940. They were slow and poorly armed for combat with high-class fighters; they carried a small bomb-load (around 2,000 pounds maximum), which they could deliver with at least a limited accuracy thanks to a system of radio navigational beams. The newest German bomber, the Junkers Ju 88A-1, could fly further, had a higher speed, and in a dive could not only bomb with greater accuracy, but could outrun a Spitfire. It was produced in small numbers in 1940, and the maximum bomb-load was only 4,000 pounds, about one-fifth of the load carried later in the war by the Avro Lancaster used in the bombing of Germany. Like all German bombers, its defensive armament was weak, and even its extra speed brought it no immunity during daylight operations against the more manoeuvrable and heavily armed British fighters.

The German Air Force also possessed a large complement of highly qualified air crew, with extensive combat experience. Although the single-engined fighter force had fewer pilots than Fighter Command, they survived longer and had a higher rate of operational readiness.[33] Most of the pilots who began the air battle had been trained well before the outbreak of war, though night-flying technique was neglected until the summer of 1940. The average age of German pilots captured in June and July was twenty-six; their average length of service was almost five years.[34] The pilots who engaged in the battle represented the cream of the German Air Force. The training system in 1940 was reformed, like the British system, to try to speed up the throughput of pilots, but standards of training were rigorous. Even if Udet had succeeded in conjuring more aircraft out of German factories, the air force would still have had difficulty supplying the men to fly them.

The task the German Air Force was called on to perform resembled, at least superficially, the opening days of the campaigns against Poland and France when the enemy air force was swiftly neutralized by concentrated bomber and dive-bomber attacks on airfields and support services. A German radio broadcast in early August explained the similarity: 'the main weapon is the bomb. German bombers will be employed with concentrated effect and in continuous waves. The effect obtained by them has already been shown in such towns as Warsaw, Rotterdam . . .'[35] German Air Force records suggest, however, that the fighter was regarded as the principal weapon. The object of the air campaign was to wipe out Fighter Command, using the bombers as bait. 'Whether the objectives were convoys in the Channel,' ran a post-war interrogation of German air leaders, 'or airfields inland, or London, the object was always the same – to bring the defending squadrons to battle to weaken them.'[36]

There was in truth a certain confusion in the instructions issued to the German Air Force in July and early

August. On 11 July the three air fleets were issued with an operational directive to begin 'intensive air warfare against England', and on 17 July they were ordered to full readiness. Probing attacks began against ports and shipping on the basis of instructions issued earlier in May, but still current, for blockade attacks on British imports. Yet another directive, issued on 16 July for Operation Sealion, ordered further preparations for invasion. Air fleets were expected to attack coastal defences, enemy troop concentrations and reserves, key communication targets and naval installations. The only object they were not yet ordered to destroy was the enemy air force, whose elimination was supposed to be the primary precondition for launching invasion at all. Only in late July did the air force commanders present to Goering their plans for winning air superiority, and not until 1 August did Hitler issue a further directive requiring the air force 'to overpower the English air force . . . in the shortest possible time' through attacks on the whole air force structure and its supporting industries. Once 'local or temporary air superiority' was gained, the air force was then expected, without explanation, to switch back to the blockade role it had started with. The knock-out blow against the RAF was set to begin on or shortly after 5 August.[37]

This plethora of orders reflected the deeper uncertainties about the conduct of the war at the highest level. The air force was much clearer in its own mind about the primary objective, and confident of achieving it. On 6 August at Carinhall, his sumptuous country estate outside Berlin, Goering had a final meeting with Kesselring, Sperrle and the commander of Air Fleet 5, General Hans Stumpff. The operational plan they adopted was straightforward: in four days Fighter Command would be destroyed over southern England. The plan was then to move forward systematically sector by sector, destroying military and economic targets up to a line from King's Lynn to Leicester, until daylight attacks could finally be extended at will over the whole of the British Isles. The initial aim was to send over small forces of bombers with a light escort, leaving the fighter force free to hunt out and destroy enemy fighters. The day for the start of the attack was codenamed *Adlertag*, day of the eagles.[38]

The precise date for the start of the campaign was more difficult to fix, since success depended critically on a spell of good weather. In Berlin the popular mood worsened at the weeks of apparent inactivity, even when skies were clear. 'Wonderful weather,' Goebbels noted acidly. 'Too good for our air force.' He detected a certain nervousness in the public: 'The people fear that we have missed the right moment.' But in Hitler he observed a real hesitancy to take 'a damn difficult decision'.[39] The date for attack was finally fixed for 10 August, but bad weather over southern England forced postponement, first to the following day, then to the morning of 13 August. The tension deepened as each day the weather intervened. 'People wait and wait for the great attack,' Goebbels noted for 12 August.[40] The following day the weather was indifferent, and attacks were postponed again until the afternoon. By chance, news of the postponement arrived too late for hundreds of aircraft already airborne. They pressed on under poor flying conditions to launch, at only part strength, the long-expected assault. *Adlertag* began not with a bang, but with a whimper.

# THREE THE BATTLE

The strength of the British fighter defence, on which the German daylight attacks and the hopes of the coveted mastery of the air had come to grief, had perhaps been underrated . . . The enemy's power of resistance was stronger than the medium of attack.

**Otto Bechtle, lecture in Berlin, February 1944**[1]

Most battles have a clear shape to them. They start on a particular day, they are fought on a geographically defined ground, they end at a recognizable moment, usually with the defeat of one protagonist or the other. None of these things can be said of the Battle of Britain. There is little agreement about when it started; its geographical range constantly shifted; it ended as untidily as it began. Neither air force was defeated in any absolute sense.

Uncertainty about when the battle started reflects the nature of the air war fought in 1940. Minor bomb attacks began on Britain on the night of 5/6 June, and small-scale, spasmodic raids continued throughout the rest of June and July. The intensification of the air assault in the second week of August prompted the Air Ministry later to assign 8 August as the start of what came to be called the Battle of Britain. When Dowding wrote his 'Despatch' in August 1941, he was reluctant to impose a neat chronology because operations 'merged into one another almost insensibly'. He rejected 8 August and suggested as the starting point 10 July, the date of the onset of heavier attacks along the Channel coast.[2] For the German side 13 August was supposed to be the day the battle for air supremacy commenced, but the attacks on that day, though larger in scale, were not regarded on the British side as a distinctive change. Air signals intelligence simply reported: 'Activity has been above normal in the past 24 hours.'[3] Even allowing for British understatement, there was little to distinguish the first days of the German assault from the previous weeks of air attack. Air Vice-Marshal Park, whose 11 Group held the front line, observed a sharp change only on 18 August, when major attacks began on fighter airfields. There may be a good case for seeing this date as the start of the decisive phase of the battle, but air fighting in defence of Britain was continuous from June onwards.

If there is no agreed date for the start of the battle, its geographical limits are also ill-defined. That this should be so does not just reflect the reality of fighting in the third dimension. German orders called for probing attacks across the British Isles against air, naval and economic targets. The attacks on 27/8 June, to take one example, were made against widely scattered cities and towns, including Liverpool, Newcastle, Scunthorpe, Southampton, Harwich and Farnborough.[4] One factor above all, however, created the elastic geography of the battle: throughout its course other RAF commands, the Royal Navy and the Germany Navy engaged in offensive operations of their own far from the air battle over southern England. These operations were intimately related to the battle. The German Navy was engaged in blockading Britain as a contribution to the effort to reduce British supplies and to encourage defeatism among the British people. The other RAF commands were employed against the threat of invasion.

The contribution of Coastal Command to the battle is all too easy to neglect. Yet the Command was given a difficult and costly responsibility. From June it mounted an anti-invasion patrol to provide intelligence on German preparations, and occasionally to engage in bomb attacks against German shipping and stores. Patrols were mounted over all German-controlled ports twice every twenty-four hours; there was continuous reconnaissance of the ports from the Hook of Holland to Ostend during the hours of darkness in case the enemy launched a surprise cross-Channel attack under cover of night. The cost was very high. Over a six-month period the Command lost 158 aircraft and 600 men from an operational strength in August 1940 of only 470 mainly obsolete aeroplanes.[5]

RAF Bomber Command was assigned an important complementary task. During the 1930s it had been assumed that in the event of all-out air war with Germany, Bomber Command would hit back in kind to deter further German attacks. Not until 15 May, following the German bombing attack on Rotterdam, was the Command given formal permission to begin operations against German territory. Its contribution was small. Poorly armed with medium bombers of limited range, Bomber Command found that the attack by day produced unacceptable, almost suicidal rates of attrition. Attacks were soon switched to night-time, and during June and July bombing of the north German coast and the Ruhr area was carried out to try to tie down the German Air Force and weaken its economic base. In July the Air Ministry developed the idea that the Striking Force, as it was known conventionally, if not entirely appropriately, should wear down German resistance 'by carefully planned bombardments of vital objectives'. If Fighter Command was the defensive guard, Bomber Command would supply 'a straight left'.[6]

If such a view was at least consistent with the familiar air force metaphor of the knock-out blow, it was utterly beyond Bomber Command's capacity or means in 1940. The directive issued on 4 July, and subsequently modified on 13, 24 and 30 July, required the bomber force to attack invasion targets in ports on the Channel coast, but also to attack a list of industrial targets regarded as decisive – aircraft production, oil, communications (power supply was added on 30 July) – and, when short of other activity, to drop incendiary pellets on flammable stretches of German forest and grainland.[7] Bomber attacks on the invasion ports, where barges and small vessels were concentrated, were carried out with modest success. The assault on German industry, power system and communications was impossible to achieve with existing technology, even if the Command had possessed adequate numbers of aircraft and sufficient pilots. During early August, however, Bomber Command suffered a greater deficiency of pilots than Fighter Command, and experienced heavy losses from operations and accidents.[8] German leaders could detect no pattern to the isolated and inaccurate attacks mounted by British bombers, and assumed that British intentions were simply to terrorize the German population.

The one field of battle where British preparations

proved at least equal to the task in 1940 was fighter defence, and it was for that reason alone that German air fleets concentrated their efforts on destroying Fighter Command. If Dowding's force had been as poorly armed and prepared as either Coastal or Bomber Command, the consequences for the future would have been far bleaker. The first phase of the air battle, in June and July, was used by the German Air Force to probe that defensive shield to see just how brittle it was. German operations took the form of regular armed reconnaissance combined with short hit-and-run attacks against widely scattered objectives by day and by night. Small numbers of bombers or dive-bombers were used, loosely protected by larger fighter screens intent on wearing down Fighter Command when the RAF flew up to engage the bombers. German targets lay mainly along the coast by day, but at night they roamed over much of Britain, bringing the bombing war to remote communities long before the Blitz, whose scale and intensity has blotted out proper recollection of the first stage of the bombing war. On 31 July, for example, bombs fell in south-east Cornwall, Somerset, Devon, Gloucestershire, Shropshire and South Wales, where Monmouth station was attacked, but little damaged.[9]

British authorities were every bit as puzzled by these attacks as the Germans were by those of Bomber

Command. German air fleets sustained regular attrition throughout the weeks of probing attacks, and achieved little serious destruction or loss of life either on the ground or against Fighter Command. The attacks certainly supplied German airmen with the opportunity to train in night-flying techniques, but they equally gave the British fighter and anti-aircraft defences weeks of precious preparation and practice, and afforded a valuable assessment of German air tactics. This learning-curve was principally of value to the defender. German fighter aircraft had developed tactics in attack that gave them the edge in combat. Flying in loose pairs, with one aircraft protecting the one in front, German fighters could fight more flexibly than the RAF, which kept fighters in tight formations of three. This tactic required a great deal of effort from the two wing aircraft to keep station with the one in the centre, and reduced the defensive assistance each could supply to the others. Such a formation was even more vulnerable if aircraft could not be alerted and sent airborne in time to get level with, or above, the enemy.

The July attacks gave Fighter Command time to iron out the teething troubles in the system of communication and to ensure that squadrons were airborne quickly and deployed economically. Gradually Fighter Command adopted the tactics of more flexible flying, and loss rates were stabilized. The probing attacks also gave the defence practice in responding to a number of different threats simultaneously, and convinced Park at 11 Group that fighters should be deployed in small formations in case attacks were mere feints, or might be followed by successive waves of aircraft. Park's policy conserved his force, though it often pitted squadrons against much larger formations of the enemy waiting on the chance to engage RAF fighters on unequal terms in large pitch battles.

What the German Air Force learned was less encouraging. German commanders hoped that bombers could be left to make their own way to targets with a loose fighter escort, which would be free to fly off to engage enemy fighters. Fighter Command, on the other hand, was obliged to fight the bombers first, as they represented the primary destructive threat. Gradually German fighters found themselves tied more closely to the bombers. The two forces, bombers and fighters, would rendezvous over the Channel and fly together, fighters slightly to the rear and from 5,000 to 10,000 feet above the bomber formations. By September German fighters were forced to fly in the front and on the flanks of the bombers to give them proper convoy protection. This tactic proved a two-edged sword, for it compelled German fighters to stick with the bombers and reduced the combat flexibility that was the distinctive strength of the German fighter arm.

It was perhaps with a sense of relief that the German Air Force finally received Goering's order to destroy Fighter Command in four days of intensive attacks in the middle of August. Bad weather interfered not only on *Adlertag* but on several subsequent days, so that the decisive shift in German strategy was obscured from the British side. Fighter Command did observe an increase in activity against radar installations from 8 August, and on fighter stations near the coast. But only by 18 August did the attack manifestly increase in intensity and move further inland against the entire structure of the fighter force.[10] Two days later, with aircraft grounded again by poor weather, Goering issued a directive to the German air fleet commanders to finish off Fighter Command with 'ceaseless attacks' by day and by night, in time for a landing in Kent and Sussex now scheduled for 15 September.[11]

The attack on Fighter Command airfields has always been regarded as the hub of the Battle of Britain. Between 12 August and 6 September there were 53 main attacks on airfields, but only 32 of these were directed at fighter stations. All but two of these attacks were made against 11 Group airfields. There were additional small raids on a wide range of lesser targets; the German Air Force calculated that there had been approximately 1,000 altogether, against industrial installations, air force supplies and communications. There were six main raids against the radar stations on the south coast, most of them on 12 August; they were not attacked repeatedly, and hardly at all towards the end of the second phase of the battle.[12] According to those attack reports that gave details of casualties, some 85 personnel were killed, at least seven of them civilians. The single largest loss of life occurred at Biggin Hill on 30 August, when 39 were killed and 25 injured in an accurate low-level bomb attack. The number of aircraft destroyed on the ground was remarkably small, and declined quickly once serious efforts were made to disperse and camouflage aircraft. Air patrols were instituted to protect refuelling squadrons from a sudden surprise attack. In total, 56 aircraft were destroyed on the ground, 42 of them in the first week of the attack, but only seven in the whole of September.[13]

The airfields that suffered severely were the group most easily reached from France. These included the forward fields at Manston, Lympne and Hawkinge near the Kent and Sussex coasts, all of which were temporarily shut down following a number of attacks. Of these Manston was the most heavily attacked, and was rendered unserviceable on six days and five nights between 14 August

and 12 September. Nevertheless, desperate efforts were made to keep airfields operational. After the first attack on Manston on 12 August, 350 men were brought in to carry out repairs and the station was operational again the following day. Aircraft were kept flying after subsequent raids until five raids in one day on 24 August left a number of unexploded bombs. This impeded full recovery for only two days.[14]

The attack on Lympne on 13 August was particularly heavy, with 400 bombs falling on the landing ground alone. Repairs were slow because construction workers had been sent to Manston to help with the attacks of the previous day. The Air Ministry sent 100 of its own building workers to help, and 150 men were found from firms in the surrounding district. When Lympne was attacked once more, on 17 August, the local men were so upset that they left, with only a small landing strip yet clear. They were induced back only to be hit by a third raid on 30 August. This time five local workers were killed when a bomb hit a slit trench; work was once more delayed. Park took the opportunity of this unfortunate history to press the Air Ministry to supply at least one bulldozer and one excavator at each aerodrome, and to allocate repair parties of 150 men from a central pool of government workers.

German Air Intelligence suggested at the end of August that at least eight airfields had been knocked out entirely and the rest of the system severely depleted. The truth was quite different. Fighter Command adapted itself quickly to the new phase of attack. Park was able to move aircraft to aerodromes further inland and to prepared satellite fields. The inland circle of airfields was then protected by the aircraft of 10 and 12 Groups, while 11 Group fighters fought the raiding aircraft. New tactics were issued to the squadrons on 19 August to cope with the airfield campaign. Fighters were told to engage the enemy over land and not risk combat over the sea, where clusters of enemy fighters waited to escort the bombers back to safety and to destroy any unwary pursuers. Pilots were encouraged to attack bombers first and avoid combat with enemy fighters, while at first notice of incoming aircraft, stations were ordered to send up a squadron to patrol below cloud cover over the airfield to minimize risk of a surprise attack. Once airborne, Spitfires were encouraged to engage enemy fighters, while Hurricanes hunted down German bombers, which may help to explain their different loss rates.[15]

The communications web held together well under the strain of attack. Sector operations rooms were out of commission on only three occasions, though the

supplementary emergency operations rooms, constructed above ground some distance from each sector station, proved inadequate as replacements. They were too cramped to house all the necessary personnel and the paraphernalia of plot tables and radio equipment; they lacked sufficient telephone landlines to operate as an integral part of the system. Radar stations emerged with remarkably little damage. The attack on Dunkirk RDF (in north Kent) destroyed two huts but inflicted no serious damage on the transmitter. The Dover station suffered slight damage to the aerial towers. At Rye, on the Sussex coast, all the huts were destroyed on the morning of 12 August, but the transmitting and receiving blocks were unscathed and operations restarted by noon. At Ventnor on the Isle of Wight all buildings were destroyed in two attacks on 12 and 16 August.[16]

If German commanders had realized sooner the role that radar played in the system, attacks might have been pressed more persistently. But because it was assumed that Fighter Command fought a decentralized battle, with squadrons tied to the radio range of their individual stations, attacks on radar were not given a high priority. They were, in any case, difficult targets to destroy completely, even more so once the Junkers Ju 87B dive-bombers were withdrawn from battle on 18 August to avoid further high losses and conserve them for the invasion. German commanders were also lulled into a false sense of security by the reports of heavy losses inflicted on the RAF in the second half of August. At the end of the month, German Air Intelligence estimated that the RAF had lost 50 per cent of its fighter force since 8 August, against a loss of only 12 per cent of the German fighter force: 791 British aircraft against 169 German. In early September, Goering was informed that Fighter Command had been reduced at one stage to a mere 100 serviceable fighters after the attacks on airfields.[17]

The real picture was remarkably different. On 23 August, Fighter Command actually had an operational strength of 672, with 228 Spitfires and Hurricanes ready in storage depots; on 1 September there were 701 operational aircraft and on 6 September the figure was 738, with 256 in stores ready for immediate despatch.[18] The losses suffered were understandably higher in late August, but the RAF daily casualty records show cumulative losses of only 444 between 6 August and 2 September, 410 of them Spitfires and Hurricanes.[19] German records of fighter losses show at least 443 for the slightly shorter period from 8 August to 31 August, with total aircraft losses during the same period standing at a little under 900.[20] Both sides made extravagant claims about the losses

inflicted on the other, largely because of double counting by pilots who could not tell clearly in the aerial mêlée who had shot an aircraft down. Yet by an odd statistical coincidence, fighter losses on the two sides were almost exactly the same in August. An evident gap opened up between the German commanders' perception of the battle and the reality facing German pilots as they engaged daily against a numerous and deadly enemy.

The assault on Fighter Command posed greater problems with the British supply of pilots. During August the casualty rate rose to 22 per cent of pilot strength, a higher rate of loss than could be made good from the Operational Training Units, which by August were turning out 320 pilots a month. A system of reinforcement was developed which gave 11 Group access to the pilots in other fighter groups. So-called 'A' squadrons were kept at full strength (20 trained pilots) and all assigned to Park's group: 'B' squadrons were kept at near full strength and assigned to other key group sectors; 'C' squadrons were set up in 12 and 13 Groups, composed of only five or six trained pilots, whose job it was to prepare the intake of operational trainees for combat in the south-east.[21] The rotation system allowed some respite to the hard-pressed front-line pilots, though it did throw into the heart of the battle less experienced crew, whose survival rates and kill ratios were lower.

These men were Churchill's 'few'. In a speech to Parliament on 20 August he repeated a sentence that he had been heard to mutter to himself a few days earlier as he returned by car from Park's headquarters at Uxbridge: 'Never in the field of human conflict was so much owed by so many to so few.' For all its subsequent reputation, the speech had, according to one of Churchill's private secretaries, 'less oratory than usual'. For much of the time 'the speech seemed to drag' in front of an audience made languid in the heat of an unaccustomed August sitting.[22] Churchill devoted only a small part of his speech to the air battle, which focused on problems in the African war against Italy; nor did he single out Britain's fighter pilots for praise. Fighter Command got six lines, but Bomber Command got twenty-one: 'On no part of the Royal Air Force,' Churchill continued, 'does the weight of the war fall more heavily than on the daylight bombers who will play an invaluable part in the case of invasion . . .'[23]

On the Fighter Command stations Churchill's remark was soon turned into a joke about mess bills. The journalists who dared the trip to these southern airfields were rewarded with scenes that have remained etched in the popular memory of the battle. 'You knew,' wrote Virginia

Cowles, looking back a year later, 'the fate of civilization was being decided fifteen thousand feet above your head in a world of sun, wind and sky.' Aircraft could be seen 'falling earthwards, a mass of flames, leaving as their last testament a smudge of black against the sky'. The pilots appeared like overgrown children, 'little boys with blonde hair and pink cheeks, who looked as though they ought to be in school'.[24] German crewmen evoked the same sentiments. When the MP Harold Nicolson saw two German Air Force prisoners at Tonbridge Station guarded by three soldiers with fixed bayonets, he thought them 'tiny little boys'. The other passengers treated them with a shy respect.[25]

The toll on the men who flew the aircraft was severe. The persistent, daily combat was physically draining and nerve-racking. Captured German prisoners at the end of August were said to show signs of 'nervous strain and cracking morale', and 'nervous exhaustion'. In his memoirs the German fighter commander Adolf Galland described the gradual demoralization of the German fighter force from the strain on minds and limbs compounded with the lack of any clear sign of operational success.[26] They at least did not suffer the indignity of being machine-gunned as they parachuted to earth. British fighter pilots were regarded as combatants as they floated down because they could be back in a cockpit within hours; German pilots could only become prisoners-of-war. Dowding in his 'Despatch' deplored the practice, but confirmed that it accorded, in his view, with the laws of war.[27]

The strain on Fighter Command crew was evident to their commanders. In August, Dowding ordered a period of twenty-four hours' rest for each pilot every week (which explained at least in part the gap between numbers available and the numbers actually flying that so enraged Churchill). In 11 Group efforts were made to repair the damage suffered by men swept round on a carousel of noise, danger and fear. Pilots were sent away to distant billets to get a night of uninterrupted sleep. More games and physical exercises were introduced. The Treasury, after much argument, finally agreed that the cost of electric lighting for airfield squash courts would be met from the public purse on the grounds, robustly argued by the Air Ministry, that a good game of squash produced a better pilot. Less energetic games were denied the public subsidy, and pilots had to pay for the lights in billiard halls out of their own pockets. Park thoughtfully arranged for airfields to be visited by string bands 'in order to remove some of the drabness of the present war'.[28]

By the beginning of September the toll was telling on both sides. Park reported to Dowding that, between 28 August and 5 September, the cumulative impact of the pounding received by airfields had had 'a serious effect on the fighting efficiency of the fighter squadrons', which could be met only by improvisation. Yet the RAF withstood the assault far better than any other air force attacked by German aircraft. The system of reinforcement was not ideal, but it provided an adequate pool of reserves, while the supply of aircraft was maintained steadily. The three airfields temporarily put out of commission had not been intended to stand in the defensive front line. They were used for the battle in France, but their proximity to the coast made them less satisfactory as defensive stations. Dowding had under his command a network of stations and satellite fields which would have kept a substantial force in contact with the attacking formations even had the forward airfields been put permanently out of action. Only a carefully directed scheme of sabotage could have disrupted the network of communications, which was limited as much by technical snags and human error as it was by the work of the enemy. Dowding commented on Park's report by pointing out that his Group had survived 40 attacks on 13 airfields, and had briefly lost the use of only three.[29] The loss rate of men and machines was as high in September when the attacks on airfields were abandoned.

At the height of this dour campaign of attrition came an intervention from Hitler which is always said to have saved Fighter Command and turned the battle. In a speech on 4 September Hitler announced that the German Air Force was to switch the main weight of attack on to British cities. London was singled out as the chief target and from 7 September, when the first mass daylight raid was launched on the capital, the German effort was concentrated on bombing the city by day and night. The respite afforded Fighter Command, so it is argued, allowed it to revive and to inflict insupportable losses on the German air fleets. The reason usually given for the sharp change in air strategy is the attack on Berlin by Bomber Command on the night of 25/26 August. Hitler was said to be so incensed by violation of the German capital that he suspended the attack on the RAF in order to unleash annihilating retaliatory blows against London; vengeance attacks made little strategic sense, and German strategy thereafter was doomed to failure.

The issues that led to the third phase of the battle were more complex than this. The central problem for Hitler and the military leadership was still to find a way to bring Britain quickly to the point where invasion could be carried out with a reasonable prospect of success. Barring invasion, there remained the hope that air attacks would prove so unendurable that the British government would at last bow to public pressure and accept the peace refused earlier in the summer. The disappointing results of the early wave of attacks in mid-August had already prompted Hitler to take stock. 'The collapse of England in the year 1940,' he told staff at his headquarters on 20 August, 'is under present circumstances no longer to be reckoned on.'[30] Nevertheless he did not cancel Sealion, nor rein back the air assault, in the hope that the situation might suddenly improve. Instead the air force moved on to the next stage of the campaign planned in July.

By late August the German Air Force commanders assumed from the intelligence they were fed that Fighter Command was a spent force. Their instructions were now to bring the rest of the country progressively under attack, starting with industrial, military and transport targets in and around major urban centres in preparation for the invasion. Heavy bomb attacks on Bristol, Liverpool, Birmingham and other Midland cities at night preceded the attacks on London. On 2 September Goering ordered the systematic destruction of selected targets in London in line with the wider aim to reduce military capability and the will to resist. On 5 September Hitler directed the air fleets to begin a general campaign against urban targets and enemy morale, including London. With this directive, according to a lecture given in Berlin later in the war, 'economic war from the air could be embarked upon with full fury, and the morale of the civilian population subjected at the same time to a heavy strain'.[31] The decision to launch attacks on London rested with Hitler, but all the preparation was in place long before. When Hitler did authorize the attack to begin, it was not a simple case of matching terror with terror, even though the first instructions to the air fleets described the operation as 'vengeance attacks'. Hitler insisted that only war-essential targets should be attacked, and rejected the idea of inducing 'mass panic' through deliberate attacks on civilian areas.[32] The raids on Berlin may have affected the timing of the decision, but even this is doubtful. At most they allowed German leaders what Goebbels described as an 'alibi': British airmen were presented in German propaganda as military terrorists, while German operations were presented as a legitimate attack on targets broadly defined as essential for war.[33]

Such a distinction is still sometimes drawn sixty years later. It is an entirely false one. The two air forces operated under almost identical instructions to hit military and economic targets whenever conditions allowed. Neither air force was permitted to mount terror attacks for the sake of pure terror. The British War Cabinet issued a directive to Bomber Command early in June 1940 instructing bomber crew over Germany to attack only when a target was clearly identified, and to seek out an alternative target in case the first was obscured. If no contact was made with the target, aircraft were expected to bring their bombs back. On moonless nights aircraft could attack 'identifiable targets in the centres of industrial activity'. With an eye to publicity (or perhaps a future war crimes trial?), the authors of the directive observed that the new requirements 'will show up quite well on the record if ever the time comes when belligerents have to produce their instructions to bombers'.[34] German airmen were also told to bomb only when they had good visual contact with the target, and to bring their bombs back if they did not. Lecture notes found on a German POW revealed detailed instructions to avoid residential districts (unless jettisoning bombs!). German airmen were told that 'on moonless nights' London could be attacked because it offered 'a large target area' in which something of value might be hit.[35]

The problem both air forces faced was the impossibility of attacking single military targets with existing air technology without spreading destruction over a wide circle around them. This explains why both sides believed that the other was conducting a terror campaign against civilian morale. By mid-September Park was telling Dowding that the Germans had abandoned 'all pretence of attacking military objectives' in favour of ' "browning" the huge London target'.[36] Goebbels invited foreign newsmen on grisly tours of bombed schools, churches and hospitals. But even he could see that journalists would not be taken in entirely by counter-claims that German aeroplanes only attacked military targets, and was even prepared to admit that it was 'impossible to avoid civilian damage'.[37] In an age long before smart weapons, accuracy to within a mile at night could be considered aerial sharp-shooting. Bombers were under constant threat of attack by fighters; they were shot at by anti-aircraft guns and trapped in cones of searchlight beams; they flew in poor daytime weather, they flew in the dark. What would now be described by the cynical euphemism 'co-lateral damage' was unavoidable, and German aircraft began to inflict civilian casualties from the moment they attacked the British mainland in June.

The claim that the attack on London was retaliation for starting an air war against civilians with the raid on Berlin on the night of 25/26 August is equally hollow. The Berlin raid was very small-scale, and the amount of damage inflicted on the capital itself negligible. The psychological impact was much greater on a population lulled into complacency by months of propaganda on the invulnerability of the city. 'The Berliners are stunned,' wrote William Shirer in his diary, 'from all reports there was a pell-mell, frightened rush to the cellars . . .'[38] On 29 August British bombers returned, this time killing ten Berliners (including four men and two women watching the pyrotechnic battle from a doorway). Goebbels made the most of a golden opportunity. 'Berlin is now in the theatre of war,' he confided to his diary. 'It is good that this is so.' The Berlin papers played up the air terror and the genocidal intention ' "to massacre the population of Berlin" '.[39]

The raids on Berlin were in reality retaliation for the persistent bombing of British conurbations and the high level of British civilian casualties that resulted. In July 258 civilians had been killed, in August 1,075; the figures included 136 children and 392 women.[40] During the last half of August, as German bombers moved progressively further inland, bombs began to fall on the outskirts of London. On the night of 18/19 August bombs fell on Croydon, Wimbledon and the Maldens. On the night of 22/23 August the first bombs fell on central London in attacks described by observers as 'extensive' and for which no warning was given; on the night of 24/25 August bombs fell in Slough, Richmond Park and Dulwich. On the night the RAF first raided Berlin, bombs fell on Banstead, Croydon, Lewisham, Uxbridge, Harrow and Hayes. On the night of the next raid on Berlin, on 28/29 August, German aircraft bombed the following London areas: Finchley, St Pancras, Wembley, Wood Green, Southgate, Crayford, Old Kent Road, Mill Hill, Ilford, Hendon, Chigwell. London was under 'red' warning for seven hours and five minutes.[41] The bombing of London began almost two weeks before Hitler's speech on 4 September, and well before the first raid on Berlin.

The switch to attacks on London forced Fighter Command and the German Air Force to rethink the battle. The main weight of German bombing slowly gravitated towards night attack, which produced much lower bomber losses. Daylight operations against the capital, which began in force on 7 September, when 350 bombers raided the east London dock area, required German fighters to fly to the very limit of their range. Bomber crews insisted that they be given an adequate defensive shield to try to reduce the heavy losses of the previous three weeks. Goering ordered fighters to fly not only in front and above the bombers, but now to weave in and out of the bomber stream itself. Because bombers were so much slower at the higher altitudes chosen for the London attacks, fighters were forced to fly a zig-zag course to keep in contact, which used up precious supplies of fuel and reduced their radius of action even more.

Fighter Command reacted to the changed battlefield almost at once. The bombers attacked London in three waves. Park ordered 11 Group to put up six squadrons held at 'readiness' for the first wave of bombers; a further eight squadrons were held back to meet the second wave; the remaining squadrons were detailed to attack the third wave, or to provide protection for airfields and factories in the bombers' path. Aircraft from 10 and 12 Groups protected 11 Group's own airfields. The higher altitude flown by the attacker added new difficulties. Radar had problems estimating the greater heights precisely; fighters had to climb further and could seldom get above the incoming aircraft, where attack was most advantageous. The problem was tackled by withdrawing from the coastal stations, to give fighters more time to assemble. When fighters were ascending, they gave false height references over the radio to bring German fighters to altitudes below them. Finally, on 21 September Park instituted standing patrols, with Spitfires flying high to engage fighters and with Hurricanes at bomber altitude.[42] The chief result of these changes was to reduce Fighter Command's loss rate and to impose escalating destruction on an already overstretched bomber force. In the first week of attacks on London, the German bomber arm lost 199 aircraft.

Over the period from 7 September to 5 October, when daylight bombing raids petered out, there were 35 major attacks, 18 of them on London. It was during this phase of the battle that the so-called 'Big Wing' controversy emerged. 'Big Wings' or 'Balbos' (after the flamboyant Italian airman Italo Balbo) were inspired by one of the legends of the battle, Wing Commander Douglas Bader. Flying with 12 Group, he developed the idea that fighters should fly in large formations in order to hit the approaching air fleet with maximum striking power. His commander, Air Vice-Marshal Leigh-Mallory, supported the innovation, but Park was strongly opposed on the grounds that concentration of fighter forces would simply let the successive waves of bombers fly on unimpeded while fighters sat on the ground rearming. What separated the two Groups were facts of geography. Park had to fight incoming waves of bombers with strong fighter escort; Leigh-Mallory's fighters met bomber forces further inland, with weaker fighter defences and their position clearly known. Under these circumstances the concentration of fighter forces made greater operational sense.

Nevertheless, as Park took pleasure in reminding Dowding, 12 Group aircraft could engage the enemy in 'Big Wings' only seldom. In September, Bader's Duxford-based squadrons flew in large formations only five times; in the second half of October they managed only ten sorties and shot down just one enemy aeroplane. In Park's judgement the use of 'Big Wings' would have 'lost the Battle of London'.[43]

The air battles in the week between 7 September and 15 September were decisive in turning the tide of the battle. During that week the German Air Force lost 298 aircraft; Fighter Command lost 120, against 99 enemy fighters. The greatest damage was inflicted on the German attack on 15 September, which has been celebrated since the war as Battle of Britain Day. A force of more than 200 German bombers, heavily escorted by fighters, attacked by day in the conventional three waves. They were met by more than 300 Spitfires and Hurricanes. A total of 158 bombers reached London, but visibility was poor and the bombs were widely scattered. The returning bombers were harried by fighters as far as the Channel. It was officially announced that night that 185 of the enemy had been destroyed. In fact during the course of the day 34 German bombers had been destroyed, 20 more extensively damaged and 26 fighters shot down. Of the original force of 200 bombers the loss rate was 25 per cent.[44] These were rates that no air force could sustain for more than a few days; they were very much greater than the worst loss rates experienced by Allied bombers over Germany in the air battles of 1943 and 1944. This was the last great daylight raid. On 18 September some 70 bombers attacked London with heavy losses. After that the attacks switched to night-time.

The fifteenth of September was also the date agreed earlier in August for the start of Operation Sealion. Enthusiasm for invasion was waning fast at Hitler's headquarters. On 30 August the date for possible invasion had been switched to 20 September to meet the navy's revised schedule. On 6 September Hitler discussed the invasion plan with Admiral Raeder. The navy took the view that Sealion was possible only if the weather and air supremacy allowed it, but Raeder began to press again for an indirect strategy. Army and navy leaders recommended a Mediterranean campaign, in collaboration with Mussolini's Italy and Franco's Spain. Hitler now faced a number of options. Sealion was not yet ruled out, though it looked an unattractive prospect in deteriorating weather; there was the possibility of destroying Britain's position throughout the Mediterranean basin and the eastern Atlantic, which would cut the Empire in two and leave Britain geographically isolated; there was a chance that the air assault on London might be 'decisive' by itself.[45]

On the afternoon of 14 September a conference assembled at Hitler's headquarters. The service chiefs were there; the issue under discussion was 'the England problem'. Hitler reminded his audience that the quickest way to end the war was to invade and occupy southern Britain. He announced that naval preparations were now complete ('Praise to the Navy,' the army chief of staff wryly noted in his war diary); he suggested that the air force campaign was poised for decisive success ('Praise above all' this time).[46] None the less, Hitler concluded that air superiority had not yet been achieved. He did not cancel Sealion, but promised to review the situation on 17 September for possible landings on 27 September or 8 October. Three days later, when the evidence was clear that the German Air Force had greatly exaggerated the extent of their successes against the RAF, Hitler postponed Sealion indefinitely. A directive on 19 September ordered preparations to be scaled down. On 12 October Hitler ordered his forces to maintain the appearance of an invasion threat in order to keep up 'political and military pressure on England'. Invasion was to be reconsidered in the spring or early summer of 1941 only if Britain had not been brought to her knees by air attack.[47]

The end of Operation Sealion in September 1940 did not end the Battle of Britain. At the meeting on 14 September Hitler gave the air force the chance to show what it could do on its own to defeat Britain: 'The decisive thing is the ceaseless continuation of air attacks.' Shortly before the meeting, Raeder had presented Hitler with a memorandum urging that air attacks 'should be intensified, without regard to Sealion'. The air force chief of staff, General Hans Jeschonnek, grasped the opportunity with both hands. He asked Hitler to allow him to attack residential areas to create 'mass panic'. Hitler refused, perhaps unaware of just how much damage had already been done to civilian targets. The air force was ordered to attack military and economic targets. 'Mass panic' was to be used only as a last resort. Hitler reserved for himself the right to unleash the terror weapon. The political will to resist was to be broken by the collapse of the material infrastructure, the weapons industry, and stocks of fuel and food. On 16 September Goering ordered the air fleets to begin the new phase of the battle. Like the campaign in Kosovo in the spring of 1999, air power was expected to deliver the political solution by undermining military capability and the conditions of daily existence.[48]

The popular fantasies of victory through air power, sustained in the 1930s by a stream of alarmist fiction (including L. E. O. Charlton's *War over England*, published in 1936, in which Britain was forced to surrender in two days after a devastating German attack on the Hendon Air Show), became a horrible truth in the last months of 1940.[49] The fear of invasion was replaced in September with a realization that Britain's population was confronted with a test of endurance for which there was no precedent. The survival of the will to fight through the period of intense bombing is now taken for granted, but it was a will that ordinary people had to find in circumstances for which no fiction can have prepared them. When the bombing began in June, Home Intelligence observers reported a general calmness, even indifference: ' "A bore rather than a terror." '[50] On a London housing estate in Stockwell, tenants busied themselves setting up home-from-home in their air-raid shelters: carpets, beds, furniture, decoration ('portraits of the King and Queen, artificial flowers, Union Jacks . . .'), and cleanly scrubbed floors. They planned an open night, 'to show off their shelter to their neighbours'. (Not everyone was so fortunate. Home Intelligence noted early in September a great many complaints about what were delicately described as ' "insanitary messes" ' and 'improper behaviour', which caused distress 'among the more respectable elements of the community'.[51]

The raids in August produced a change in mood. With the intensification of bomb attack, Home Intelligence found that morale stiffened; the spirit of those in raided areas was regarded as 'excellent', the shock of war on the home front even produced a temporary exhilaration. London came through its first weekend of raids 'with confidence and calmness' (though the inhabitants of Croydon were reportedly 'resentful' when the all-clear sounded just ten minutes before German bombers appeared overhead to disgorge their loads).[52] In August the author John Langdon-Davies rushed out a booklet which he titled *Nerves versus Nazis*. It was marketed as a manual for 'successful mental counter-attack' against air raids, and Langdon-Davies wrote it after watching '400 typical Londoners' descend to their shelters with 'no fear, no panic'. He offered advice on coping with fear, which included his own practice of 'counting slowly from the moment that I hear the first bomb. If I count up to 60 and am still counting, then I know that I have survived . . .' He encouraged his readers to buy a large-scale local map, mark their own house with a blue dot, stand on a chair with 50 grains of salt and drop them on the plan. The reader would then be reassured by the discovery that 'most of the salt grains have not hit any building at all . . . it will be a strange mischance if any grain of salt has actually hit the blue pencil point, which marks your own home'.[53]

When the bombing began on a large scale in early September, the strain of constant attack began to tell. Home Intelligence found that in the aftermath of the raids on London's docks there was more evidence of panic and mass evacuation, of 'nerve cracking from constant ordeals'.[54] It is no reflection on the courage or powers of endurance of the bombed populations that they sought a way out of the turmoil. In a great many cities refugees from bombing spread out into the surrounding countryside. At the end of September it was reported that it was 'practically impossible to get a room anywhere within seventy miles of London'. The heavy raids on Plymouth and Southampton left thousands of people living in tents and rough camps on the outskirts. Thousands of Londoners left for destinations they believed safer. In the East End there were widespread anti-semitic rumours about Jews who fled first and fastest, or sat in air-raid shelters all day.[55] Even the West End was not immune from such prejudices. When the author George Orwell heard the rumours, he went to investigate a sample of underground stations converted to bomb shelters by night: 'Not all Jews,' he noted in his diary, 'but, I think, a higher proportion of Jews than one would normally see in a crowd of this size. What is bad about Jews is that they are not only conspicuous, but go out of their way to make themselves so.'[56]

By late September the initial panics had died down; small thanks, perhaps, to Langdon-Davies. 'Morale in general continues good,' ran the Home Intelligence weekly report. This was attributed in official circles either to the fact that 'the more depressed have evacuated themselves', or to the discovery that air raids 'are not so terrible once you have got used to them'.[57] It owed something to the fact that the threat of German invasion was now palpably receding. Rumours of invasion had surfaced throughout the summer and autumn, most of them in areas very remote from the south coast. The military authorities were themselves exposed to regular invasion scares from a variety of intelligence sources. The Joint Intelligence Committee reported early in July that full-scale invasion could be expected at any time from the middle of the month, but the chiefs of staff took the view that invasion would only come after the air battle, and no further alert was issued until early September when photographic reconnaissance and isolated items of Enigma information suggested the concentration of German forces opposite the south coast. On 7 September the codeword CROMWELL was issued to prepare all home-based forces for immediate action.[58]

The Air Ministry had provided a key numbered 1–3 for different states of readiness (1 = attack improbable, 2 = attack probable, 3 = attack imminent); on 27 August the key was suddenly reversed to make 1 the more dangerous option. On 7 September code 1 was activated for an invasion 'likely to occur in the next twelve hours'. Some stations failed to get the alert at all; others still used the old 1–3 code.[59] Even if the alert had been properly managed, Fighter Command was entirely absorbed by the air defence battle, and would have been severely pressed to fight off invasion at the same time. The weekend of 14–15 September was popularly regarded as 'Invasion Weekend' because of the conjunction of favourable tides and a full moon. On the south coast the fields and farmyards filled with troops ordered to sleep with their boots on. When nothing happened, alert no. 2 was issued, only for 'invasion imminent' to be reinstated on 22 September. Only on 25 October was no. 3 introduced permanently, by which time fragments of intelligence from Europe indicated that invasion was no longer likely.

During October and November, bombing replaced invasion as the chief public concern. 'There is neither fear nor expectation of invasion,' ran the Home Intelligence report for the third week of October. After two months of bombing there was evidence of a strong desire to restore some sense of normality in cities where bombing occurred only seldom, and where damage was less than at first feared. Even in London, where there were 24 attacks in September, and an attack every night during October, the maintenance of daily life was a key to survival and a weapon against demoralization. The familiar images of workers and shoppers picking their way through bomb debris each morning is mute testimony to the efforts made to reassert the rhythms of ordinary life. The *Daily Express* ran a campaign under the caption 'Don't be a Bomb Bore'. When the Ministry of Information began to compile lists of 'Questions the Public Are Asking' in October, the newsletters were full of mundane inquiries: 'Are animals allowed in shelters?'; 'Are people liable to pay rent and rates if their houses are made uninhabitable?'; was there compensation for the loss of 'false teeth, spectacles, gas masks . . . ?'[60]

There was little evidence of widespread hatred of the enemy, however understandable it might have been. Violence erupted briefly against Italian premises in London in June when Italy entered the war (one Italian grocery, the Spaghetti House, hastily changed its name to British Food Shop).[61] Home Intelligence found that public calls for bombing reprisals were directed against Italy as much as Germany. There was surprisingly slender evidence of sustained Germanophobia. The call for reprisals died down in October, but was more marked in areas where there had been no bombing. The Ministry of Information observed in November that populations that had not experienced raids 'seem more prone to exaggeration and self-pity than others who have been badly bombed'. In one opinion poll carried out in the north-east, only 58 per cent favoured bombing reprisals against Germany. Earlier in the summer the Ministry had begun an orchestrated campaign to 'stir up the people's more primitive instincts'. Some uncertainty prevailed about how to do this, and the propagandists were left with the unhelpful conclusion that it was 'merely sufficient to impress the people that they were in fact angry'. The campaign was quietly dropped.[62]

The transfer to night bombing in September altered the nature of the aerial battlefield once again. Fighter Command was responsible for the night-fighter force, made up predominantly of Blenheims and Beaufighters, but in the absence of adequate aerial radar to find bombers in the dark, contact with night raiders was largely accidental. At night the anti-aircraft defences were the main line of defence. When concentrated attacks began on London, guns were brought in from other parts of

Britain to provide a more satisfactory barrage. Anti-aircraft batteries claimed 337 aircraft destroyed from July to September, but of those only 104 were at night, when it was estimated that a barrage used up to ten times as many shells per aircraft as visual firing.[63] The reality was that aircraft were very difficult to shoot down at night from the air or from the ground until the advent of new detection equipment. German air fleets found that half their casualties from October onwards were caused by accidents resulting from poor weather conditions and ice.

By day the bomber force gradually disappeared. It was substituted by large formations of fighters, a small group converted to a fighter-bomber role with the addition of one 250 kg bomb, and an escort of between 200 and 300 combat fighters. The shift had two purposes. First, fighter bombers could keep up the pressure on the urban population by regular small-scale attacks which strained already jangled nerves; second, the fighter sweeps were intended to engage Fighter Command in a steady war of attrition to try to complete the process of wearing down the fighter force begun in July. The strategy made sense only in the light of the persistent misrepresentations of Fighter Command strength by German Air Intelligence, which continued to assert that the enemy was down to its last 200–300 aircraft and that British aircraft production was falling sharply under the hail of bombs. In October, 253 of the nuisance raids were mounted; in November, 235.[64] Aircraft flew at altitudes well above 20,000 feet, where the Me 109 was at an advantage thanks to its two-stage engine supercharger. At such heights the slow ascent from RAF airfields to meet the enemy proved a grave handicap and loss ratios began to favour the attacker.

Fighter Command switched tactics once more. Standing patrols of high-flying Spitfires were used to reconnoitre incoming fighter sweeps. On sighting the enemy, other fighter squadrons patrolling at lower altitudes flew up to battle stations. Air fighting at high altitude brought new difficulties. British aircraft did not have pressurized cabins and the hood was prone to leak at altitude, inducing terrible cramps for the unfortunate pilot. Fighting at high altitude was more physically draining, particularly for RAF squadron commanders whose average age was almost thirty. Losses in October totalled 146 Hurricanes and Spitfires; German air fleets lost 365 aircraft, of which a high proportion were bombers subject to increasingly hazardous flying in the late autumn nights.[65] Nevertheless the loss of pilots in Fighter Command was down to only 10 per cent of the force in October, and in November losses of both aircraft and pilots fell to a new low point as the daylight air battle died away as falteringly and inconclusively as it had started.

From October the German leadership placed its faith in the political impact of bombing for want of any other form of direct pressure on Britain. Some airmen favoured a short and brutal campaign of terror against British cities and food supplies to bring a swift capitulation, along the lines first outlined by the Italian General Giulio Douhet in his classic study of air power published in 1921, *Command of the Air*. The 'England-Committee' of Ribbentrop's foreign office also strongly favoured a short terror campaign to drive the inhabitants of the East End of London across what they called the 'social fault line' into the West End, where London's well-to-do would be frightened into making peace from fear of social revolution.[66]

Though the German Air Force never formally adopted terror bombing, the tactics of widely scattered attacks, the use of a special incendiary squadron to start fires for other bombers to follow, the relaxation of rules of engagement over London on moonless nights, the deliberate decision to target the enemy psychologically by attacking intermittently round the clock (and for as long as possible at night), the use of aerial mines and the targeting of administrative areas of the capital, all reveal the gradual abandonment of any pretence that civilians and civilian morale would not become targets. The death of more than 40,000 people during the Battle of Britain and the Blitz may not have been deliberate policy, but must surely stretch the idea of 'co-lateral damage' beyond the limits of meaning. In Berlin Goebbels gloated in his diary almost daily throughout the last months of 1940 over the horrors of air warfare. 'When will Churchill capitulate?' he asked in November. On 5 December he noted the frightful reports from Southampton: 'The city is one single ruin . . . and so it must go on until England is on her knees, begging for peace.' On 11 December Goebbels heard Hitler address the Party bosses: 'the war is militarily as good as won . . . England is isolated. Will bit by bit be driven to the ground.'[67]

# FOUR A VICTORY OF SORTS

I think we have managed to avoid losing this war. But when I think how on earth we are going to win it, my imagination quails.

**Harold Nicolson, diary, 8 November 1940**[1]

We shall win, but we don't deserve it; at least we do deserve it because of our virtues, but not because of our intelligence.

**Winston Churchill, 10 August 1940**[2]

Britain was not driven into the ground in 1940 and Germany did not win the war. These statements are commonplace enough. The difficulty is to decide what, if anything, connects them, for the Battle of Britain did not seriously weaken Germany and her allies, nor did it much reduce the scale of the threat facing Britain (and the Commonwealth) in 1940/41 until German and Japanese aggression brought the Soviet Union and the United States into the conflict. The issues in 1940 cannot be reduced to a simple dividing line between victory and defeat.

In the first place the threat from the German Air Force was just one of the problems Britain faced in the autumn and winter of 1940. The war against Italy in north and east Africa was a major contest, whose outcome was just as critical for the long-term survival of Britain's global imperial position. In August Italian armies invaded Somaliland, and in September crossed into Egypt. The large Italian Navy forced Britain to fight a major naval campaign in the Mediterranean at a time when ships were desperately needed for defence against invasion and to protect the vital trade routes across the Atlantic on which Britain's long-term survival depended. This war against Italy exposed how fragile Britain's position was in 1940, fighting two European great powers, her navy under constant submarine threat, the economy in crisis, a predatory Japan in eastern Asia, waiting for Britain's star to fall like France before her. In the end only a small portion of the war effort of Britain and the Commonwealth was exerted against the German Air Force in the autumn war in the air.

The German threat itself was only partly reduced as a result of the air battles. In late November 1940 a pessimistic Churchill was reportedly still anxious that Germany 'will strive by every means to smash us before the Spring'.[3] The one thing that the Battle of Britain could not prevent was the bombing. Even during the daylight clashes between July and September, a high proportion of bombers reached and bombed their targets. German air fleets could not bomb at will, and they sustained what proved to be debilitating loss rates by day, but there was no effective way of preventing bombing, even when the navigational beams were finally jammed by British counter-measures in November. The factors that undermined the effectiveness of the bombing campaign both by day and by night were self-inflicted: bomb attacks were carried out with small bomb-loads, with relatively small numbers of aircraft, and over a widely scattered number of targets. Many of these targets were of secondary importance; no target system, whether airfields, communications, ports or industry, was attacked repeatedly, systematically or accurately. When British Air Intelligence analysed the German bombing effort in late September 1940, they found the results 'remarkably small in proportion to the considerable effort expended'. In the absence of any observably consistent bombing strategy, the British concluded that the German Air Force bombed 'with the primary object of lowering morale', which it failed to do in any significant sense.[4]

The onset of the bombing war in September 1940, the 'Blitz' as it soon became known, revived anxieties about a sudden overwhelming strike from the sky to force surrender on a stunned people. When Harold Nicolson visited the Master of Corpus Christi College in Cambridge in January 1941, he was warned that the public had no idea 'how gigantic the German knock-out blow will be when it comes'.[5] Gas warfare was a persistent fear. In November the Labour Leader Clement Attlee was given responsibility to get Britain's stock of poison gas up to the level of 2,000 tons agreed before the war, in case the Germans used gas as a final resort. Churchill became more anxious as time passed that desperation might push the enemy to resort to chemical weapons. In February 1941 a cypher message arrived from Budapest, courtesy of the American legation, warning not only that the invasion of Britain was scheduled for March, but also that German scientists had perfected 'a new soporific gas' whose effects would last for thirty-six hours whilst German forces stormed ashore. To Churchill's immediate inquiry about Britain's gas capability, the Air Staff replied that the RAF could attack the German population with gas bombs for only four or five days, but if gas was mixed in with high-explosive bombs the campaign might last for two or three weeks.[6]

That same month came further intelligence from Switzerland that Germany had retained a secret force of 10,000 aircraft to hit Britain with one massive aerial blow at a critical moment. Churchill now asked the Air Staff to tell him what kind of aerial 'banquet' the RAF could lay on in retaliation. Though the RAF was rightly sceptical about any secret air force, they relayed to Churchill the

cheerless statistical conclusion that Germany could probably send across some 14,000 aircraft, while the RAF
could scrape together only 6,514, including 2,000 trainers
and 3,000 reserves.[7]

The edginess evident among British political circles
reflected the widespread belief that invasion had only
been postponed in September 1940 by the exertions of
Fighter Command, not cancelled. In the spring of 1941
the Ministry of Information renewed the circulation of
pamphlets about invasion in an effort to challenge popular complacency; Fighter Command was issued with new
operational instructions early in March for the fight over
the invasion beaches. Information from Europe was
ambiguous, partly because Hitler had ordered a campaign
of deception to mask the operational preparations to
attack the Soviet Union by apparently maintaining the
pressure on Britain; and partly because Hitler did not
entirely exclude the possibility of invasion if Britain
became sufficiently weakened or demoralized. In discussion with the German Navy commander in January,
he suggested that the aerial and naval blockade of British
imports might lead to victory as early as July or August
1941, or create the conditions necessary to permit successful invasion and occupation, or, finally, produce the
coveted 'negotiated' peace.[8]

It is evident that Hitler's view of the British problem did not alter a great deal between the summer of 1940 and the spring of 1941. The air battles of August and September 1940 were regarded from the German side as just one part of a campaign that lasted almost a year to find ways of bringing sufficient pressure on Britain to get her to give up. The campaign included a political offensive to persuade Spain and Italy to collaborate in destroying Britain's precarious military position in the Mediterranean and North Africa (an effort that stumbled on Franco's refusal to join the war, and Mussolini's decision, kept secret from Hitler, to move into the Balkans instead by invading Greece in October 1940). The naval war, which grew into what became known as the Battle of the Atlantic, developed as a blockade strategy largely independent of the invasion operation, and one that pushed the British war effort to its limit long after the Battle of Britain. Invasion itself was always just one option, and one for which Hitler himself had deep reservations.

It is open to debate whether the air battle of the autumn of 1940 was the decisive factor affecting the German decision whether or not to invade. There were other reasons for delaying. It is often forgotten that there stood more than an air force between Hitler and conquest of

Britain. The German Navy was heavily outnumbered by the Royal Navy, even one stretched taut by the demands of other theatres. The German Navy as a result always remained half-hearted about the whole operation, and made its views felt throughout the weeks of preparation. The British army may not have been a match for the German army in the field, but it also represented a considerable threat to a landing attempt. The German army leadership undertook what preparations they could, but they were faced with an operation for which there was simply no precedent in German military history, and one for which preparation was at best improvised. General Günther von Blumentritt, an army staff officer assigned to Operation Sealion, later described the preparations carried out in 1940 as woefully inadequate: 'It must not be forgotten that we Germans are a continental people,' he wrote. 'We knew far too little of England. We knew literally nothing of amphibious operations. At the time we were preparing Sealion plans accounts of the campaigns of Caesar, Britanicus and William the Conqueror were being read . . .'[9] Above all, the German leadership recognized, as the western Allies were to realize in the invasion of Normandy four years later, that defeat would be a political and military catastrophe. 'It is imperative,' wrote General Alfred Jodl, Hitler's Chief of Operations, in August 1940, 'that no matter what might happen the operation dare not fail.'[10]

There need be no doubt that under the right circumstances Hitler was serious about invading Britain in 1940. There remained, none the less, a genuine ambivalence in his attitude to the British problem. He understood how difficult the practical questions were and was keen to avoid 'risky experiments' and 'high losses'. He confessed to an audience of Party bosses that he was 'shy of the water', which may explain why he listened so closely to what Raeder and the navy had to say in 1940.[11] He wanted invasion to be foolproof, 'absolutely assured'. He kept the door open to a political settlement: 'Even today the Fuehrer is still ready to negotiate peace with Britain,' ran the minutes of a Führer conference in January 1941.[12] Hitler's view of Britain is well known: a curious blend of envy and admiration, of contempt for her current state of decadence and respect for a famous history. In his memoirs Adolf Galland recalled a conversation with Hitler when he came to Berlin from the air battle in September 1940 to collect Germany's highest military award, the oak leaves to the Knight's Cross. Alone with Hitler, Galland told him the unalloyed truth about how tough air combat against Britain had proved to be. Instead of the diatribe of contradiction he had expected, Hitler explained his respect for the Anglo-Saxon peoples, his regret at the life-and-death struggle between the two states – the 'world-historical tragedy' that now promised only total destruction where there might have been fruitful collaboration.[13]

It is evident that not a lot was needed to deter Hitler from the idea of invading Britain. Fighter Command tipped the scales. The failure to destroy the Royal Air Force ruled out the possibility of a cheap, quick end to the war in the west and kept alive an armed anti-Axis presence in Europe. The full significance of this outcome was not realized on the British side as the air battle shifted to its new and more deadly phase from September 1940. But when Dowding forwarded to the Air Ministry in mid-November a report on the previous two months of air fighting compiled by Air Vice-Marshal Park, he began at last to develop some sense of what his force had now achieved:

. . . the point to remember is that the losses sustained by the enemy were so great that heavy day attacks by bombers were brought to a standstill and that the Command did, in fact, win a notable victory; since, if the attacks had not been brought to a standstill, the invasion would have been facilitated and the war might well have been lost.[14]

It is this achievement that came to be described as the Battle of Britain.

Victory in this narrow but important sense has been explained in many ways. German airmen were at a disadvantage attacking over enemy territory with very limited fighter range. Fighter Command was able to draw on the resources of the other nine-tenths of the British Isles outside the range of the Me 109. Even if the forward airfields had been lost permanently, British fighter forces could still have been deployed from bases further inland, though they might then have taken a lower toll of the enemy bomber force. The German fighter force became tied to the bomber stream as the battle drew on, limiting its radius of action and manoeuvrability without affording the bombers real security from attack on the way out or the way back. All the time Fighter Command was improving the means to identify and engage the enemy through radar and signals intelligence.

In a great many respects, however, the two forces were remarkably matched. Both commanded a small group of committed, highly trained and courageous pilots; both forces responded with considerable tactical ingenuity to sudden changes of direction in the course of the battle; both exploited fighter aircraft at the cutting edge of aviation technology; both forces fought the battle with operational commanders of real distinction – Dowding and Park, Kesselring and Sperrle. There were periods in the battle that favoured the German side, others in which Fighter Command began to exact a higher toll. Every small technical or tactical drawback suffered by one force can be matched by problems experienced by the other.

The contest was not, of course, a draw. German air fleets did not gain air supremacy over southern Britain, for all their skill and technical competence. Two factors gave the edge to the RAF: the balance of forces between the two sides, and the role of intelligence. For the whole of the battle period, the British aircraft industry outproduced the German by a considerable margin. This allowed a continuous flow of replacements to compensate for the higher loss rates sustained by Fighter Command. The Command grew steadily stronger between June and October. On 19 June there were 548 operationally ready fighters (with 200 more ready for the following day); on 31 October there were 729 ready to fly, 370 in store at a day's notice, and a further 110 at four days'.[15] German levels of production and serviceability were too low to establish an effective numerical superiority. German fighters flew in large groups with the bombers, which gave an impression of overwhelming numbers, while Fighter Command aircraft were divided between Groups, not all of which were in the front line. But Dowding's system of rotation ensured that most squadrons saw service in southern England, and that each German attack was met in sufficient force to exact casualties.

The balance of pilots was also more favourable than the legend of the 'few' suggests. German single-engined fighter pilots available for the battle remained below the British figure throughout the three months of combat. The impact of regular fighting under difficult conditions eroded combat numbers. At the beginning of September only 74 per cent of German fighter pilots were operationally ready, and that month pilot losses reached almost one-quarter of the force, 23.1 per cent.[16] Moreover, and importantly, German pilots and aircrew were lost to the battle if they were shot down and captured on British soil. Between 1 July and 31 October, 967 prisoners were taken and 638 bodies definitely identified. The POWs were found to be experienced pilots. Only two had been trained since the war. The oldest was fifty-one years old, a veteran of the First World War; the oddest was the 47-year-old Oberleutnant Haffl von Wedel, a Berlin history professor recruited to write the air force official history, who was permitted to fly in combat to give his scholarship a practical foundation. He was shot down on his twenty-fourth mission.[17] The pre-war origin of the pilot population suggests that the German Air Force suffered the loss during the battle of a high proportion of its cadre force. Nor was there to be any heroic break-out from POW camps; three-quarters of those captured were shipped overseas to Canada.[18]

The true balance of forces was never properly understood on either side. The result was a mutual misperception that played a critical part in the conduct of the battle. Throughout the summer, indeed ever since the outbreak of war, German Air Intelligence, run by Colonel Josef 'Beppo' Schmidt, had greatly *under*estimated the size of the RAF and the scale of British aircraft production. Across the Channel the Air Intelligence division of the Air Ministry consistently *over*estimated the size of the German air enemy and the productive capacity of the German aviation industry. As the battle was fought, both sides exaggerated the losses inflicted on the other by an equally wide margin. However, the intelligence picture formed before the battle encouraged the German Air Force to believe that such losses pushed Fighter Command to the very edge of defeat, while the exaggerated picture of German air strength persuaded the RAF that the threat it faced was larger and more dangerous than was actually the case.

German misperception encouraged first complacency,

then strategic misjudgement. The shift of targets from air bases to industry and communications was taken because it was assumed that Fighter Command was virtually eliminated. On 16 September, the day after the mauling inflicted on the daylight bomber raids against London, Goering announced that Fighter Command had just 177 operational aircraft left. German Air Intelligence estimated that there were only 300 British fighters left altogether, including reserves, and a monthly output of 250. On 19 September Fighter Command had an actual operational strength of 656; there were 202 aircraft in immediate reserve, 226 in preparation; output of fighters between 7 September and 5 October was 428.[19] The discrepancy was critical. German airmen were ordered to fight in September as if Fighter Command had been all but eliminated; the reality was a level of attrition so high that the German Air Force could not sustain it for more than a few weeks. The casualties of this paradox were German aircrew who fought a battle that bore little relation to the one their commanders told them to expect.

Fighter Command, on the other hand, could not afford to be complacent. The high losses inflicted on the German Air Force reduced the threat, but as long as it was assumed that the enemy was much stronger there could be no question of relaxing any particle of effort. In the western intelligence community there existed a profound misapprehension of the scale and character of the German air fleets, even though by August details were being supplied regularly from 'Ultra' decrypts of German Air Force Enigma traffic. For a long time it was assumed that each German squadron was stronger than it actually was because the balance between reserves and operational aircraft had not been properly understood. American air intelligence officers calculated German aircraft output at around 26,000 in 1940, rising to 42,000 in 1941, with at least 31,000 pilots trained between July 1939 and December 1940 to fly them; German first-line combat strength was estimated at 11,000, with 100 per cent reserves. British estimates were more modest than this: Air Intelligence suggested output of 24,400 aircraft in 1940, and a front-line strength of 5,800 in August. The true figures were far below these estimates. Aircraft output was in fact only 10,247 in 1940 and 12,401 in 1941; German Air Force first-line strength in September 1940 was 3,051 aircraft of all types, of which 2,054 (68 per cent) were serviceable. Of this figure approximately 80 per cent was used for the assault on Britain.[20] Some intelligence estimates were better than others (the Ministry of Economic Warfare was spot on with an estimate of 3,000 front-line strength, but was disregarded by the airmen). Not until the spring of 1941 did estimates begin to approach reality. The British fought the air battle as if it were a last-ditch struggle against an overwhelming enemy; the German side fought against a force persistently misrepresented as technically and tactically inept, short of aircraft, pilots and bases. This psychological contrast put the German Air Force at a perpetual disadvantage.

The German failure to win air supremacy was beyond doubt by October as the air conflict slowly subsided. Neither side was defeated in any conventional sense. Though the battlefield was littered with the debris of combat, the two fighter forces in October each had around 700 operational aircraft and sufficient numbers of trained pilots to fly them, a balance of forces not very different from the start of the battle. German losses greatly exceeded those of the RAF because of the vulnerability of bombers and dive-bombers. Between 10 July and 31 October the RAF lost 915 aircraft, the German Air Force 1,733. Losses on both sides were soon made good. The outcome was technically a stalemate. British forces had little prospect of re-entering Continental Europe; German forces could not, under present circumstances, invade or occupy Britain.

The public was at first only dimly aware of the significance of the battle they had witnessed day after day, framed against the autumn skies. When Orwell read the official narrative in April 1941, he was surprised by 'the way in which "epic" events never seem very important at the time'.[21] The conflict was not yet presented as the familiar Battle of Britain. When Churchill used the term in a speech in June, he was referring to the whole field of conflict, not simply to the battles of air defence. When the speech was reprinted later in the year, the Battle of France was capitalized, but the 'battle of Britain' was not. Park talked about the Battle of London; the army commander-in-chief of Southern Command, General (later Field Marshal) Alexander thought that the heavy night bombing in the winter heralded the onset of what he called the 'Battle of England'.[22]

The lack of any clear sense that a great battle had been won was reflected in the treatment of those who had won it. The fighter aces for the most part remained anonymous because the RAF wanted to avoid the pitfalls of glamorizing a few heroes at the expense of the rest of the force. Once the daylight battles were over, the commanders who brought victory were dispensed with. Throughout the battle a backstairs intrigue was conducted against Newall and Dowding, involving, among others, the veteran airman Lord Trenchard and the Minister of Aircraft Production, Lord Beaverbrook. A whispering campaign against Newall's alleged incompetence, begun by a junior officer in the Air Ministry, reached Sinclair and Churchill. Enough of the mud stuck. On 2 October it was decided that Newall should be replaced by Air Marshal Sir Charles Portal. Dowding in the meantime found himself once again at odds with the Air Staff, who believed that he was not taking effective action against German night-bombing. Despite Churchill's support for him earlier in the year, the political pressure to get rid of the man who had just led Fighter Command to victory became irresistible. Dowding was finally replaced in November by Sholto Douglas. He departed under a cloud; he was posted to America to help promote Britain's campaign for economic aid, but he was not a success. He retired in 1941 to indulge his enthusiasm for paranormal phenomena.[23]

The Air Ministry decision to publish a publicity pamphlet on the air battles finally gave the conflict the narrative shape it had hitherto lacked. The *Battle of Britain*, a 32-page account of the air battle, was produced in March 1941. More than a million copies were sold in Britain alone. It was printed and distributed separately in the United States and the Dominions. The Ministry chose 8 August as the date the battle started, and 31 October was selected arbitrarily for the end. More than anything else, *Battle of Britain* gave the conflict the legendary dimensions it has borne ever since. Dowding was not involved, or even mentioned in the text. He was supposed to have been invited to write his own despatch on the air operations, but the Ministry forgot to authorize it. Only later in 1941, when Churchill asked to see what Dowding had written, did the Ministry invite him to offer his views on the battle. The 'Battle of Britain Despatch' was completed in August 1941. A year later Churchill asked once again what impact the despatch had had when it was distributed, only to be told that it had been too sensitive a document to circulate beyond a select few in the Ministry.[24] Dowding's views on the battle, which were a good deal more hard-headed than those presented in the Air Ministry pamphlet, were locked away until the war was over.

One of the purposes in producing the pamphlet was for propaganda, particularly in the United States where the battle had attracted less attention than the Blitz. The images of blazing London filed by American journalists, along with poignant eye-witness accounts of the bombing, stirred popular opinion, though it did not bring the United States any nearer to belligerency. The battle had less resonance abroad, in part because it was just one corner of a larger canvas of war. The American public maintained a lively scepticism over the claims made about German aircraft losses, and Churchill in August 1940 thought about banning American journalists altogether from the field of battle.[25] The American public was more interested in the Japanese war with China and the war at sea, and leaders and led alike were absorbed in Roosevelt's efforts to be elected president for an unprecedented third term. Many influential Americans came to favour giving Britain economic assistance, but in government circles the view still circulated that Britain might well be defeated as France had been, and American goods fall into the wrong hands. In August, at the height of the air battle, the most important issue in Anglo-American relations was the argument over the precise terms of the deal to give Britain 50 destroyers in exchange for American bases on British colonial territory. Even a lifeline as slender as this was interpreted at home and abroad as a symbol of America's willingness to support the efforts of an embattled sister democracy. Yet in the long run, as Churchill rightly recognized, Britain's successful defiance of Germany made possible American's later entry into Europe, without which Britain's hope of victory was slight.

The Battle of Britain mattered above all to the British people, who were saved the fate that overtook the rest of Europe. The result was one of the key moral moments of the war, when the uncertainties and divisions of the summer gave way to a greater sense of purpose and a more united people. This was a necessary battle, as Stalingrad was for the eastern front. In June Kenneth Clark reported to the Ministry of Information the effects of a recent morale campaign. He confessed that the campaign had not been a success: 'people do not know what to do ... difficulty arose in satisfying the people that the war could be won'.[26] By November the mood was less desperate. A Gallup Poll showed 80 per cent of respondents confident that Britain would win in the end. Ministry informers reported a widespread desire to end the propaganda 'Britain can take it' and to substitute the slogan 'Britain can give it!'[27]

Even civilians enjoyed the sense that they, too, could contribute directly to the war effort through their own sacrifices and endeavours. There emerged an evident mood of exhilaration when the population found itself fighting at last after months of inactivity. Men flocked in thousands to join the Local Defence Volunteers, though they were poorly organized and scarcely armed by the time invasion was likely: many would have been treated, as the German side made clear at the time, as irregular militia, subject to summary execution. The Battle of Britain and the Blitz that followed contributed to the growing sense that this was a people's war. There is more than a touch of irony that the battle was actually won by a tiny military elite, and at the cost of only 443 pilots.[28] The heroic defences on the eastern front, of Moscow and Sevastopol and Stalingrad, cost the defender, soldier and civilian, millions of war dead. The efficiency of Britain's defensive effort in 1940 was one of its most remarkable features. The 'few' did indeed save the many from a terrible ordeal.

The air battles were necessary to rouse the self-belief and staying power of a people demoralized by the sudden collapse of democratic Europe in the summer of 1940. No one pretends that the Battle of Britain decided the war, or that it papered over all the cracks that appeared in British morale and outlook in 1940. With hindsight it might have been fought more effectively, though British air defences were manifestly better organized than most other areas of Britain's war effort. The cost of losing the battle would have spelt national disaster. No appeasing peace with Hitler could have masked the reality of defeat. The Battle of Britain was the first point since 1931, when Japan occupied Manchuria, that the forces of violent revision in world affairs were halted. In a radio broadcast in 1942, George Orwell reminded his listeners that Trafalgar Day had just been celebrated. He suggested that Trafalgar played the same part in the Napoleonic wars 'as the Battle of Britain in 1940 occupied in this one'. In both cases invasion and defeat would have meant a Europe 'given over to military dictatorship'. After Trafalgar the invasion scare subsided 'and though it took another ten years to win the war, it was at any rate certain that Britain could not be conquered at one blow'.[29] To the British people, then and now, that was sufficient.

**NOTES**

The following abbreviations have been used throughout
the Notes:

ADAP:    *Akten zur deutschen auswärtigen Politik*
AHB:     Air Historical Branch, Ministry of Defence, London
BA-MA:   Bundesarchiv-Militärarchiv, Freiburg
CAS:     Chief of Air Staff
COS:     Chiefs of Staff
FCNA:    *Führer Conferences on Naval Affairs, 1939–1945*
         (London, 1990)
GAF:     German Air Force
IWM:     Imperial War Museum, London
OKW:     Supreme Command of the Armed Forces
PRO:     Public Record Office, Kew, London
RAF:     Royal Air Force
RDF:     Radio Direction Finding

## ONE THE SETTING

**1** PRO AIR 14/381, Plan W1, 'Appreciation of the Employment of the British Air Striking Force', April 1938, p. 1.

**2** R. Rhodes James (ed.), *'Chips': The Diaries of Sir Henry Channon* (London, 1993), p. 215; gas masks in PRO INF 1/264, Home Intelligence, summaries of daily reports, 28 March 1940.

**3** K.-H. Völker, *Dokumente und Dokumentarfotos zur Geschichte der deutschen Luftwaffe* (Stuttgart, 1968), doc. 200, pp. 469–71.

**4** PRO AIR 1/5251, report by the Brooke-Popham Committee, 16 July 1940, p. 3.

**5** PRO AIR 14/181, Commander, Advanced Air Striking Force to Bomber Command HQ, 5 March 1940; AIR 9/117, Anglo-French staff conversations, 'The Attack of German Railway Communications', 26 April 1939.

**6** AHB, 'Battle of Britain: Despatch by Air Chief Marshal Sir Hugh Dowding, 20 August 1941' (hereafter: AHB, Dowding 'Despatch'), p. 8.

**7** PRO CAB 120/294, Air Ministry report to War Cabinet, 24 June 1940; German losses in N. L. R. Franks, *The Air Battle of Dunkirk* (London, 1983), p. 194. British losses over Dunkirk totalled 177, including 106 fighters: see R. Jackson, *Air War Over France May–June 1940* (London, 1974), p. 121.

**8** Lloyd George in G. Eggleston, *Roosevelt, Churchill and the World War II Opposition* (Old Greenwich, Conn., 1979), p. 130; Churchill speech in M. Gilbert (ed.), *The Churchill War Papers*, vol. 2 (London, 1994), p. 368.

**9** R. A. Callahan, *Churchill: Retreat from Empire* (Delaware, 1984), p. 79; P. Addison, 'Lloyd George and Compromise Peace in the Second World War', in A. J. P. Taylor (ed.), *Lloyd George: Twelve Essays* (London, 1971), p. 381.

**10** PRO PREM 7/2, letter from Foreign Office to Desmond Morton, 28 May 1940.

**11** PRO INF 1/264, Home Intelligence daily reports: 28 May 1940, p. 1; 31 May 1940, p. 1.

**12** Addison, 'Lloyd George', pp. 365, 378; A. Roberts, *The 'Holy Fox': A Biography of Lord Halifax* (London, 1991), p. 243.

**13** PRO INF 1/878, War Cabinet conclusions, 18 May 1940, p. 3.

**14** PRO PREM 7/2, note from Morton to Churchill, 30 May 1940, enclosing note by Cadogan dated 25 May 1940.

**15** PRO INF 1/264, Home Intelligence daily reports, 17 June 1940.

**16** PRO INF 1/264, Home Intelligence daily reports, 17 June, 18 June, 20 July 1940.

**17** PRO AIR 9/447: War Ministry, Plans Division, 'Eire', 31 May 1940, pp. 1–3; COS meeting on home defence, 7 July 1940.

**18** PRO AIR 9/447, Air Ministry minute, 20 June 1940.

**19** PRO INF 1/849, Ministry of Information, Policy Committee: meeting of 8 July 1940, p. 2; meeting of 23 July 1940; meeting of 24 July 1940; INF 1/264, Home Intelligence daily reports, 20 July 1940. See too D. Cooper, *Old Men Forget: The Autobiography of Duff Cooper* (London, 1953), pp. 286–7.

**20** V. Cowles, *Looking for Trouble* (London, 1941), pp. 416–17.

**21** W. Boelcke (ed.), *The Secret Conferences of Dr Goebbels* (London, 1970), p. 60, meeting of 3 June 1940.

22 H.-A. Jacobsen (ed.), *Generaloberst Halder: Kriegstagebuch* (3 vols, Stuttgart, 1963), vol. 2, pp. 30–31, entry for 22 July 1940.

23 *FCNA*, pp. 110–11, 'Conference with the Führer', 20 June 1940; Jacobsen (ed.), *Kriegstagebuch*, p. 3, entry for 1 July 1940.

24 *ADAP*, Serie D, Band X, p. 56, minute of state secretary, 30 June 1940.

25 IWM, EDS collection, OKW Aktennotiz, 'Chefbesprechung', 12 June 1940.

26 *ADAP*, Serie D, Band X: p. 105, Schulenburg to German Foreign Office, 5 July 1940; pp. 202–3, Prince Max von Hohenlohe to German Foreign Office, 18 July 1940; p. 216, Dublin Embassy to German Foreign Office, 22 July 1940.

27 M. Muggeridge (ed.), *Ciano's Diary, 1939–1943* (London, 1947), p. 275, entry for 7 July 1940.

28 *FCNA*, pp. 116–17, Directive 16, 'Preparations for the Invasion of England'.

29 M. Domarus, *Hitler: Reden und Proklamationen 1932–1945* (3 vols, Munich, 1963), vol. 2, pp. 115–18; W. Shirer, *Berlin Diary: The Journal of a Foreign Correspondent, 1934–1941* (London, 1941), pp. 355–8.

30 Shirer, *Berlin Diary*, pp. 355–6.

31 On Halifax see Roberts, *'Holy Fox'*, p. 249; on Berlin see Shirer, *Berlin Diary*, p. 360.

32 See J. Förster, 'Hitler Turns East – German War Policy in 1940 and 1941', in B. Wegner (ed.), *From Peace to War: Germany, Soviet Russia and the World, 1939–1941* (Oxford, 1997), pp. 117–24; E. M. Robertson, 'Hitler Turns from the West to Russia,

May–December 1940', in R. Boyce (ed.), *Paths to War: New Essays on the Origins of the Second World War* (London, 1989), pp. 369–75.

## TWO THE ADVERSARIES

1 PRO AIR 22/72, Air Ministry weekly intelligence summary, report for 18 July 1940, p. 4.

2 *FCNA*, pp. 124–5, 'Conference with the Führer', 31 July 1940.

3 M. Dean, *The Royal Air Force and Two World Wars* (London, 1979), pp. 100–101.

4 Details in R. Wright, *Dowding and the Battle of Britain* (London, 1969), pp. 73–6, 138–44.

5 PRO PREM 3/29, summarized order of battle, 19 June 1940, 9 August 1940.

6 AHB, 'The Battle of Britain: A Narrative Prepared in the Air Historical Branch', n.d., p. 574.

7 PRO AIR 22/293, Cabinet Statistical Branch, 'Statistics on Aircraft Production, Imports and Exports, Schedule D, Exports of Fighters'.

8 PRO AIR 22/493, Schedule C, weekly imports April–November 1940.

9 PRO AIR 8/372: War Cabinet conclusions, 22 May 1940; minute, Chief of Air Staff, 22 May 1940; Cripps to the War Cabinet, 26 June 1940.

10 PRO AIR 16/365, 'Fighter Command, Operational Strength of Squadrons and Order of Battle'.

11 PRO AIR 22/262, 'Daily Returns of Casualties to RAF Aircraft', 25 June–29 September 1940.

12 AHB, Dowding 'Despatch': p. 27; on self-sealing tanks, Appendix F. See too PRO AIR 16/715, HQ no. 24 Training Camp to HQ Fighter Command, 1 October 1940, 'Notes of Conversations with Fighter Pilots'.

13 PRO AIR 22/296, Cabinet Statistical Branch, 'Personnel: Casualties, Strength, Establishment of the RAF'; W. Murray, *Luftwaffe: Strategy for Defeat, 1933–1945* (London, 1985), p. 54; C. Webster and N. Frankland, *The Strategic Air Offensive against Germany 1939–1945* (4 vols, London, 1961), vol. 4, p. 501, Appendix 49 (xxviii).

14 PRO AIR 8/463, Air Intelligence, 'Present and Future Strength of the German Air Force', November 1940.

15 PRO PREM 7/2: Churchill to General Hastings Ismay, 26 June 1940; War Cabinet Polish Forces Committee, meeting of 1 July 1940; 'Minute, Position of the Polish Air Force in England', 30 June 1940. On efforts to find pilots, see AIR 6/70, Air Council minutes, 23 July, 6 August, 22 August 1940; AIR 19/162, Churchill to Sinclair, 12 August 1940.

16 PRO AIR 22/296, 'Casualties, Strength, Establishment of the RAF'; AIR 16/659: for Churchill's comment see Churchill minute, 24 June 1940 for Ismay; Fighter Command to Ismay, 27 June 1940. It took only three minutes to refuel a fighter, but ten minutes to rearm it.

17 AHB, Dowding 'Despatch', pp. 11–12.

18 PRO CAB 120/309, 'Notes of Meeting, 16 September 1940, on Inland Looking'; on the Observer Corps see D. Wood and D.

Dempster, *The Narrow Margin: The Battle of Britain and the Rise of Air Power, 1930–1940* (London, 1961), pp. 153–8.

**19** S. Cox, 'A Comparative Analysis of RAF and Luftwaffe Intelligence in the Battle of Britain, 1940', *Intelligence and National Security*, 5 (1990), pp. 432–4; F. H. Hinsley et al., *British Intelligence in the Second World War*, vol. 1 (London, 1979), pp. 177–82.

**20** Details in AHB, Dowding 'Despatch', p. 10. A 'Purple' warning was later added at night to warn services such as stations and docks to extinguish all work-essential lighting as an attacking force approached. Cooper's remark in PRO INF 1/849, Policy Committee meeting, 1 July 1940. On anti-aircraft defences see B. Collier, *The Defence of the United Kingdom* (London, 1957), pp. 153–4.

**21** PRO AIR 9/136, Air Ministry, draft memorandum, 'Measures to be Taken in the Event of a German Invasion of England', 29 October 1939, pp. 1–8.

**22** PRO AIR 16/212, Fighter Command operational instructions, 8 July 1940, pp. 1–8; operational instructions, 18 September 1940, pp. 2–4.

**23** PRO AIR 9/136, 'Measures to be Taken . . .', p. 2.

**24** PRO WO 199/22, report for GHQ Home Forces, 31 July 1940, prepared by Major-General B. Taylor; Commander, London area, to GHQ Home Forces, 24 August 1940. Despatch, p. 18.

**25** PRO PREM 3/88 (3), War Cabinet, COS memorandum, 'Plans for Employment of Gas from the Air in Retaliation for its Use against Us by the Enemy', 8 October 1940; AIR 9/136, Air Ministry memorandum, 'Bomber and Fighter Efforts Available to Counter an Attempted Invasion', 5 March 1941.

26 PRO AIR 9/447, Air Ministry, Plans Division: draft directive to Air Officer Commanding in Ireland, 24 June 1940; 'Minute from Director of Plans', 2 June 1940.

27 W. Green, *Warplanes of the Third Reich* (London, 1970), p. 544.

28 *The Rise and Fall of the German Air Force, 1933–1945* (London, 1983, reprinted from AHB narrative, 1948), pp. 75–6.

29 Pre-war planning in National Archives, microcopy T177, roll 31, 'Nachschubzahlen für Luftfahrtgerät', 1 April 1938 (which estimated output of 1,753 per month on mobilization). Plans 15 and 16 in BA-MA, RL3 159, Lieferprogramm Nr 15, 1 September 1939, and Flugzeug-Beschaffungs-Programm Nr 16, 28 October 1939. The 1940 plan in BA-MA, RL3 162, Lieferplan Nr 18, 1 July 1940.

30 British figure from PRO AIR 22/293, 'Statistics: Aircraft Production, Imports and Exports, Schedule B' (production from 1 June to 30 September).

31 D. Irving, *The Rise and Fall of the Luftwaffe: The Life of Erhard Milch* (London, 1973), p. 136.

32 PRO AIR 16/635, HQ 11 Group to HQ Fighter Command, 7 November 1940, 'German Attacks on England 11 September–31 October 1940', pp. 6–9.

33 Murray, *Luftwaffe*, pp. 54–5; Webster and Frankland, *Strategic Air Offensive*, vol. 4, p. 501.

34 PRO AIR 22/72, Air Ministry weekly intelligence summary, 8 August 1940, p. 3.

35 PRO AIR 22/72, weekly summary, 15 August 1940, p. 4.

36 AHB, 'Battle of Britain' narrative, Appendix 37, 'German

Views on the Battle of Britain', p. 1 (based on interviews with Field Marshal Erhard Milch and General Adolf Galland).

**37** H. Trevor-Roper (ed.), *Hitler's War Directives 1939–1945* (London, 1966), pp. 74–9, Directive 16, 16 July 1940; pp. 79–80, Directive 17, 1 August 1940. AHB, 'The Course of the Air War against England', translation of German AHB study, 7 July 1944, pp. 1–2.

**38** PRO AIR 40/2444, O. Bechtle lecture, 'German Air Force Operations against Great Britain, Tactics and Lessons Learned 1940–1941', 2 February 1944, pp. 2–4.

**39** E. Fröhlich (ed.), *Die Tagebücher von Joseph Goebbels: Sämtliche Fragemente* (4 vols, Munich, 1987), vol. 3, pp. 264, 270, 271.

**40** Goebbels, *Tagebücher*, p. 277.

## THREE THE BATTLE

**1** PRO AIR 40/2444, Bechtle lecture, pp. 7–8.

**2** AHB, Dowding 'Despatch', p. 5.

**3** PRO AIR 22/478, RAF Wireless Intelligence Service, daily summary, 13 August 1940. See too AIR 22/72, Air Ministry weekly intelligence summary, 15 August 1940, p. 1 – activity was 'much higher than had been normal'.

**4** PRO AIR 16/432, report on enemy activity over Great Britain, 27/28 June 1940.

**5** C. Goulter, *A Forgotten Offensive: Royal Air Force Coastal Command's Anti-Shipping Campaign 1940–1945* (London, 1995), pp. 111–22.

6 PRO AIR 9/447, Air Ministry, Director of Plans, memorandum, 'Employment of the Air Striking Force', 8 July 1940.

7 Webster and Frankland, *Strategic Air Offensive*, vol. 4, pp. 118–24.

8 PRO AIR 22/296, 'Casualties, Strength and Establishment of the RAF'. In mid-August the deficiency of bomber pilots reached a peak of 219; the highest deficiency of fighter pilots was 181 on 24 August.

9 PRO AIR 16/432, Home Security intelligence summary, 31 July/1 August.

10 PRO AIR 16/216, HQ 11 Group to all Group controllers, 19 August 1940.

11 AHB, 'Course of the Air War . . .', p. 2; *FCNA*, p. 128, OKW directive, 16 August 1940.

12 AHB, 'Battle of Britain' narrative, Appendix 8 III, 'Table of Chief Attacks on Airfields and RDF Stations', pp. 1–9.

13 AHB, 'Battle of Britain' narrative, Appendix 34 II, 'Fighter Command Aircraft Destroyed or Damaged on the Ground'.

14 This paragraph and following account in PRO AIR 16/635, 'Notes of Damage and Repairs at Certain Fighter Aerodromes', 21 September 1940.

15 PRO AIR 16/216: HQ 11 Group to all Group controllers, 19 August 1940; telegram from 11 Group HQ to all airfields, 20 August 1940.

16 AHB, 'Battle of Britain' Narrative, Appendix 8 III.

17 Jacobsen (ed.), *Kriegstagebuch*, vol. 2, p. 81, entry for 30 August 1940; *Rise and Fall*, p. 85.

18 PRO AIR 22/293, Schedule E, 'Number of Aircraft in Storage

Units'; PREM 3/29 (3), summarized order of battle, 6 September 1940; AIR 16/635, Fighter Command HQ, operational strength, 1 September 1940.

19 PRO AIR 22/262, 'Daily Return of Casualties to RAF Aircraft', 25 June–29 September 1940.

20 *Rise and Fall*, pp. 82–3; see too O. Groehler, *Geschichte des Luftkriegs* (Berlin, 1981), p. 272, for figures on aggregate German losses.

21 AHB, Dowding 'Despatch', pp. 21–4.

22 J. Colville, *The Fringes of Power: 10 Downing Street Diaries 1939–1945* (London, 1985), p. 227, entry for 20 August 1940. Colville confessed in a footnote that he did not even notice the sentence when he sat listening to the speech. The invention of the remark can be found in J. Winant, *A Letter from Grosvenor Square: An Account of a Stewardship* (London, 1947), pp. 29–30.

23 Gilbert, *Churchill War Papers*, pp. 693–4, speech to the House of Commons, 20 August 1940.

24 Cowles, *Looking for Trouble*, pp. 424–6.

25 N. Nicolson (ed.), *Harold Nicolson: Diaries and Letters 1939–1945* (London, 1967), p. 111, entry for 7 September 1940.

26 PRO AIR 8/315, Chief of the Air Staff, 'Analysis of the G. A. F. Personnel Losses, July–October 1940'; AIR 22/72, Air Ministry weekly intelligence summary, report for 12 September 1940, p. 3; A. Galland, *The First and the Last* (London, 1955), p. 34.

27 AHB, Dowding 'Despatch', p. 20.

28 AHB, Dowding 'Despatch', p. 24; PRO T265/19, Treasury Inter-Service Committee, meeting of 3 October 1940 for final decision; AIR 16/635, HQ 11 Group to HQ Fighter Command,

7 November 1940, 'German Attacks on England 11 September–31 October', p. 14.

**29** PRO AIR 16/635, HQ 11 Group to HQ Fighter Command, 12 September 1940, pp. 6–7; Dowding to Air Ministry, 22 September 1940, 'German Attacks on England 8 August–10 September', pp. 1–2. See too AHB, Dowding 'Despatch', pp. 18–19.

**30** IWM, EDS documents, AL 1492, OKW Aktennotiz, 20 August 1940.

**31** PRO AIR 40/2444, Bechtle lecture, p. 4; K. Maier, 'Die Luftschlacht um England', in *Das deutsche Reich und der zweite Weltkrieg*, vol. 2 (Stuttgart, 1979), p. 386. See too J. Ray, *The Night Blitz 1940–1941* (London, 1996), pp. 97–102.

**32** Jacobsen (ed.), *Kriegstagebuch*, p. 100, entry for 14 September 1940.

**33** Goebbels, *Tagebücher*, p. 313.

**34** PRO AIR 9/447: COS meeting, 'Bombardment Policy', June 1940; Air Ministry, Director of Plans, memorandum, 8 July 1940.

**35** PRO AIR 40/2444, Bechtle lecture, p. 5; AIR 22/72, Air Ministry weekly intelligence summaries, 8 August, 12 September 1940.

**36** PRO AIR 16/635, HQ 11 Group to HQ Fighter Command, 12 September 1940, p. 5.

**37** Goebbels, *Tagebücher*, p. 315, entry for 9 September 1940.

**38** Shirer, *Berlin Diary*, pp. 381, 384.

**39** Goebbels, *Tagebücher*, p. 296, entry for 27 August 1940; Shirer, *Berlin Diary*, p. 384.

**40** Maier, 'Luftschlacht', p. 405.

41 PRO AIR 16/432, Home Security intelligence summaries, reports of operations, 24/25 August, 25/26 August, 28/29 August.

42 PRO AIR 16/635: HQ 11 Group to HQ Fighter Command, 7 November 1940, pp. 1–5; HQ 11 Group to HQ Fighter Command, 12 September 1940, pp. 4–6; AHB, Dowding 'Despatch', pp. 11–12.

43 PRO AIR 16/635, HQ 11 Group to HQ Fighter Command, 7 November 1940, pp. 3–4, 12.

44 Bekker, *Luftwaffe Diaries*, p. 226; Collier, *Defence of the United Kingdom*, pp. 244–5.

45 *FCNA*, pp. 133–5, 'Conference with the Führer', 6 September 1940; p. 136, Naval Staff memorandum, 10 September 1940. Maier, 'Luftschlacht', pp. 386–7.

46 Jacobsen (ed.), *Kriegstagebuch*, vol. 2, pp. 98–9, entry for 14 September 1940.

47 *FCNA*, pp. 136–9: 'Conference with the Führer', 14 September 1940; OKW directive, 19 September 1940; OKW directive, 12 October 1940. Jacobsen (ed.), *Kriegstagebuch*, vol. 2, p. 99.

48 *FCNA*, p. 137, memorandum from Admiral Raeder, 14 September 1940; Jacobsen (ed.), *Kriegstagebuch*, vol. 2, p. 100; Maier, 'Luftschlacht', pp. 390–91.

49 L. E. O. Charlton, *War over England* (London, 1936), pp. 158–81.

50 PRO INF 1/264, Home Intelligence daily reports, 27 June 1940.

51 PRO INF 1/264, reports for 28 June, 6 September 1940.

52 PRO INF 1/264, report for 23 August 1940.

53 J. Langdon-Davies, *Nerves versus Nazis* (London, 1940), pp. 7, 14, 17–18.

54 PRO INF 1/264, Home Intelligence daily reports, 6 September 1940.

55 PRO INF 1/264, reports for 9, 10 September 1940.

56 G. Orwell, 'War-time Diary: 1940', entry for 25 October 1940, in *The Collected Essays, Journalism and Letters* (4 vols, London, 1968), vol. 2, pp. 427–8.

57 PRO INF 1/292 Part I, Home Intelligence weekly reports, report for 30 September–9 October, p. 1.

58 Hinsley, *British Intelligence*, vol. 1, pp. 172–3, 184–5.

59 PRO AIR 16/356: Air Ministry to Dowding, 1 August, 27 August 1940; cypher messages, Fighter Command, 7 September, 22 September, 24 September, 13 October, 25 October.

60 PRO INF 1/283, Ministry of Information newsletter, 'Questions the Public Are Asking', 23 September, 9 October; Cowles, *Looking for Trouble*, p. 446.

61 Orwell, 'War-time Diary: 1940', p. 394.

62 PRO INF 1/292 Part I, Home Intelligence weekly report, 4 November–11 November 1940, pp. 1–2; INF 1/849, Ministry of Information Policy Committee, meeting of 4 June 1940, p. 1.

63 AHB, Dowding 'Despatch', Appendix C.

64 AHB, 'Course of the Air War', p. 3.

65 PRO AIR 22/263, 'Daily Returns of Casualties to RAF Aircraft', 29 September 1940–31 January 1941; AIR 16/635, HQ 11 Group to HQ Fighter Command, 7 November 1940, 'German Attacks on England 11 September–31 October 1940', pp. 6–12; German figures in Groehler, *Geschichte des Luftkriegs*, p. 272.

**66** Maier, 'Luftschlacht', p. 392; Groehler, *Geschichte des Luft-kriegs*, p. 270.

**67** Goebbels, *Tagebücher*: p. 429, entry for 12 December 1940; p. 410, entry for 24 November; p. 420, entry for 5 December 1940.

## FOUR A VICTORY OF SORTS

**1** H. Nicolson, *Diaries and Letters*, p. 126, letter from Nicolson to Vita Sackville-West, 8 November 1940.

**2** Colville, *Fringes of Power*, p. 266.

**3** Nicolson, *Diaries and Letters*, p. 129, diary 22 November 1940.

**4** PRO AIR 22/72, Air Ministry weekly intelligence summary, 19 September 1940, pp. 4–5.

**5** Nicolson, *Diaries and Letters*, p. 140, diary 23 January 1941.

**6** PRO PREM 3/88 (3): Churchill to Ismay, 26 December 1940; cypher message from Mr O'Malley, Budapest, 4 February 1941; Portal (CAS) to Churchill, 13 February 1940.

**7** PRO AIR 8/463, Portal to Churchill, 18 February 1941, 20 March 1941.

**8** PRO AIR 9/136, Air Ministry memorandum, 'Bomber and Fighter Efforts Available to Counter Attempted Invasion', 5 March 1941; *FCNA*, p. 172, 'Conference with the Führer', 8/9 January 1941.

**9** G. Blumentritt, 'Operation "Sealion"', in D. Detweiler (ed.), *World War II German Military Studies* (24 vols, New York, 1979), vol. 7, pp. 10–11.

**10** H. Greiner, 'Operation Seelöwe and Intensified Air Warfare against England up to October 30 1940', in Detweiler, *German Military Studies*, vol. 7, p. 10.

**11** Goebbels, *Tagebücher*, p. 429, entry for 12 December 1940.

**12** *FCNA*, p. 172, 'Conference with the Führer', 8/9 January 1941.

**13** Galland, *First and Last*, p. 45.

**14** PRO AIR 16/635, Dowding to Air Ministry, 15 November 1940, p. 2.

**15** PRO PREM 3/29 (3), summarized order of battle, 31 October 1940.

**16** Murray, *Luftwaffe*, p. 54.

**17** PRO AIR 22/72, Air Ministry weekly intelligence summary, 26 September 1940; AIR 8/315, CAS, 'Analysis of GAF Personnel Losses', July–October 1940.

**18** PRO 8/315, War Cabinet to CAS, 29 August 1940.

**19** Maier, 'Luftschlacht', p. 391; PRO AIR 16/365, Fighter Command operational strength, 19 September 1940.

**20** Library of Congress, Washington DC, Arnold Papers, Box 246: Chief of Intelligence memorandum, 'Estimate of German Air Strength', 21 January 1941, enclosing G2 report, 'Germany, Domestic Production, Capacity and Sources of Aviation Equipment', 16 January 1941, pp. 1–9. PRO AIR 8/463: CAS memorandum, 'Strength of the GAF', 8 July 1940; 'Present and Future Strength of the German Air Force', 1 December 1940, pp. 1–3.

**21** Orwell, 'War-time Diary: 1941', p. 443, entry for 8 April 1941.

**22** R. Churchill (ed.), *Into Battle: Speeches by the Right Hon. Winston S. Churchill* (London, 1941), p. 234, speech broadcast 18 June 1940; Nicolson, *Diaries and Letters*, p. 132, diary 31 December

1940; PRO AIR 16/635, HQ 11 Group to HQ Fighter Command, November 1940, p. 4.

**23** See S. Ritchie, 'A Political Intrigue against the Chief of the Air Staff: The Downfall of Air Chief Marshal Sir Cyril Newall', *War & Society*, 16 (1998), pp. 83–104.

**24** PRO AIR 19/258, letter from Air Ministry to Sinclair, 5 April 1941, for details on the pamphlet; on the Despatch see AIR 2/7771, circulation list for Dowding's Despatch, 14 September 1941, CAB 120/311: Churchill to Sinclair, 15 June 1941; Churchill to Portal, 23 August 1942; Portal to Churchill, 27 August 1942.

**25** PRO CAB 120/294, Churchill to Sinclair, 21 August 1940. See N. J. Cull, *Selling War; The British Propaganda Campaign against American 'Neutrality' in World War II* (Oxford, 1995), ch. 3.

**26** PRO INF 1/849, Ministry of Information Policy Committee, meeting of 21 June 1940, p. 1.

**27** PRO INF 1/292, Home Intelligence weekly report, 18–24 December 1940, p. 1.

**28** PRO AIR 22/100, 'Fighter Command Daily Casualties'. From 1 July–1 November 1940 the Command lost 284 pilots killed on operations and 159 killed in accidents.

**29** W. J. West, *Orwell: The War Commentaries* (London, 1985), pp. 168–9, broadcast 24 October 1942.

# TABLES AND MAPS

# The Hurricane and the Spitfire:
# Production, Operational Strength and Losses

**Table 1:** Production per week, June–November 1940

| Date | Hurricanes | Spitfires |
|------|------------|-----------|
| 1–7 June | 87 | 22 |
| 8–14 June | 79 | 22 |
| 15–21 June | 67 | 25 |
| 22–28 June | 75 | 21 |
| 29 June–5 July | 68 | 26 |
| 6–12 July | 65 | 32 |
| 13–19 July | 57 | 30 |
| 20–26 July | 67 | 41 |
| 27 July–2 August | 65 | 37 |
| 3–9 August | 58 | 41 |
| 10–16 August | 54 | 37 |
| 17–23 August | 43 | 31 |
| 24–30 August | 64 | 44 |
| 31 August–6 September | 54 | 37 |
| 7–13 September | 54 | 36 |
| 14–20 September | 56 | 38 |
| 21–27 September | 57 | 40 |
| 28 September–4 October | 58 | 34 |
| 5–11 October | 60 | 32 |
| 12–18 October | 55 | 31 |
| 19–25 October | 55 | 25 |
| 26 October–1 November | 69 | 42 |
| **Total** | **1,367** | **724** |

**Table 2:** Operational strength: number of squadrons, July–October 1940

| Date | Hurricane squadrons | Spitfire squadrons |
|---|---|---|
| 14 July 1940 | | |
| 10 Group | 2 | 2 |
| 11 Group | 12 | 7 |
| 12 Group | 6 | 5 |
| 13 Group | 5 | 5 |
| **Total** | **25** | **19** |
| 1 September 1940 | | |
| 10 Group | 4 | 4 |
| 11 Group | 14 | 6 |
| 12 Group | 6 | 6 |
| 13 Group | 9 | 2 |
| **Total** | **33** | **18** |
| 30 September 1940 | | |
| 10 Group | 6 | 3 |
| 11 Group | 13 | 7 |
| 12 Group | 6 | 6 |
| 13 Group | 9* | 3 |
| **Total** | **34** | **19** |
| 28 October 1940 | | |
| 10 Group | 6 | 3 |
| 11 Group | 13 | 8 |
| 12 Group | 7 | 6 |
| 13 Group | 7** | 3 |
| **Total** | **33** | **20** |

*includes 2 half-strength squadrons    **includes 1 part-strength squadron

**Table 3:** Operational losses per week, July–November 1940 (aircraft totally destroyed)

| Date | Hurricanes | Spitfires |
|---|---|---|
| 10 May–29 July | 173 | 110 |
| 30 July–5 August | 2 | 9 |
| 6–12 August | 47 | 25 |
| 13–19 August | 84 | 38 |
| 20–26 August | 39 | 33 |
| 27 August–2 September | 96 | 48 |
| 3–9 September | 86 | 53 |
| 10–16 September | 50 | 24 |
| 17–23 September | 21 | 19 |
| 24–30 September | 60 | 29 |
| 1–7 October | 17 | 19 |
| 8–14 October | 21 | 19 |
| 15–21 October | 18 | 14 |
| 22–28 October | 22 | 16 |
| 29 October–4 November | 17 | 11 |
| **Total** | **753** | **467** |
| (as percentage) | 61.7 | 38.3 |

Sources:

Table 1: PRO AIR 22/293, 'Weekly Output of Fighters'.

Table 2: PRO AIR 16/365, 'Fighter Command, Operational Strength of Squadrons and Order of Battle'.

Table 3: PRO AIR 22/262, 'Daily Returns of Casualties to RAF Aircraft', 25 June–29 September 1940.

# Single-engined Fighter Pilot Strength, RAF and German Air Force

**Table 1:** Fighter Command pilot strength

| Week ending | Establishment | Operational strength |
|---|---|---|
| 30 June 1940 | 1,482 | 1,200 |
| 27 July 1940 | 1,456 | 1,377 |
| 17 August 1940 | 1,558 | 1,379 |
| 31 August 1940 | 1,558 | 1,422 |
| 14 September 1940 | 1,662 | 1,492 |
| 28 September 1940 | 1,662 | 1,581 |
| 19 October 1940 | 1,714 | 1,752 |
| 2 November 1940 | 1,727 | 1,796 |

**Table 2:** German Air Force, single-engined fighter pilot strength

| Date | Fully operational pilots |
|---|---|
| 1 June 1940 | 906 |
| 1 August 1940 | 869 |
| 1 September 1940 | 735 |
| 1 November 1940 | 673 |

Sources:

Table 1: PRO AIR 22/296, 'Personnel: Casualties, Strength and Establishment of the RAF'.

Table 2: C. Webster and N. Frankland, *The Strategic Air Offensive against Germany* (4 vols, London, 1961), vol. 4, p. 501; W. Murray, *Luftwaffe: Strategy for Defeat 1933–1945* (London, 1985), p. 54. For September, Webster and Frankland give a figure of 688 operational pilots.

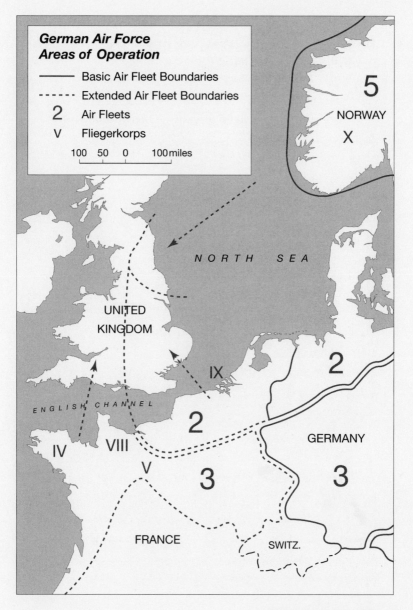

German Air Force
Areas of Operation

——— Basic Air Fleet Boundaries
----- Extended Air Fleet Boundaries
2 Air Fleets
V Fliegerkorps

100 50 0 100 miles

NORWAY

NORTH SEA

UNITED KINGDOM

ENGLISH CHANNEL

GERMANY

FRANCE

SWITZ.

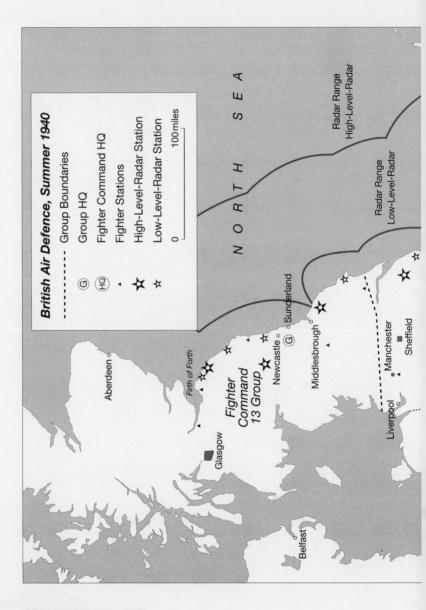

British Air Defence, Summer 1940

Group Boundaries
Group HQ
Fighter Command HQ
Fighter Stations
High-Level-Radar Station
Low-Level-Radar Station

0    100 miles

NORTH SEA

Radar Range
High-Level-Radar

Radar Range
Low-Level-Radar

Aberdeen

Firth of Forth

Fighter
Command
13 Group

Glasgow

Newcastle

Sunderland

Middlesbrough

Belfast

Liverpool

Manchester

Sheffield

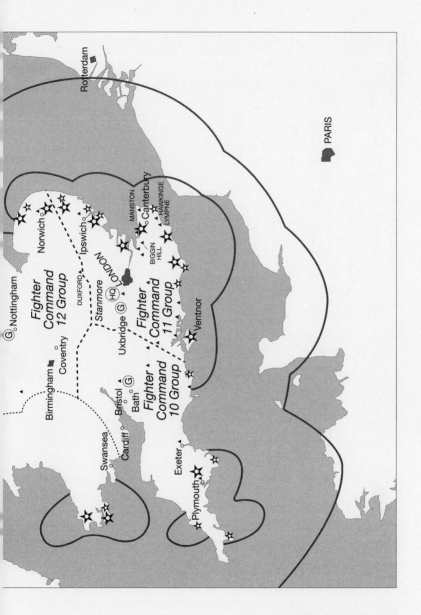

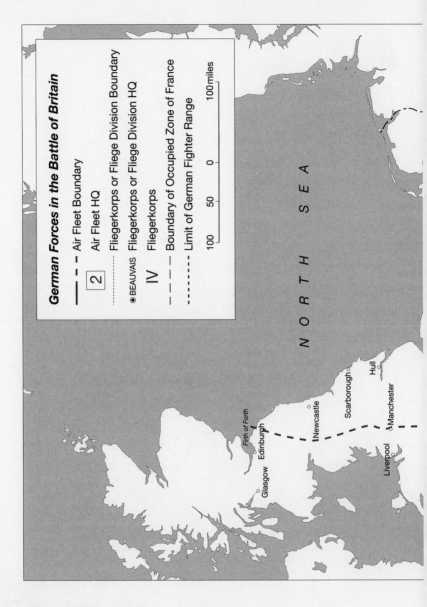

German Forces in the Battle of Britain

Air Fleet Boundary

2 Air Fleet HQ

Fliegerkorps or Fliege Division Boundary

⊙BEAUVAIS Fliegerkorps or Fliege Division HQ

IV Fliegerkorps

Boundary of Occupied Zone of France

Limit of German Fighter Range

100   50   0   100miles

NORTH SEA

Firth of Forth

Glasgow
Edinburgh

Newcastle

Scarborough

Hull

Liverpool

Manchester

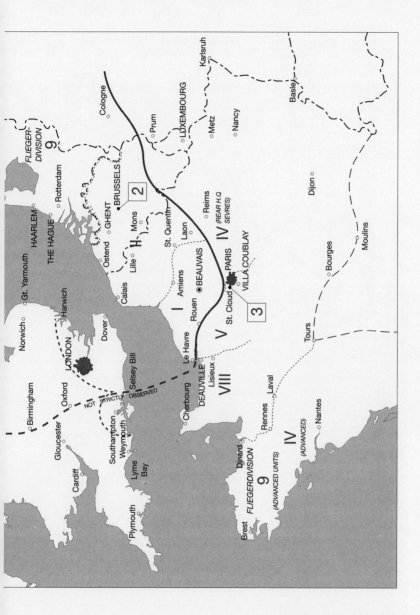

**INDEX**

Adlertag, 62–3
Advanced Air Striking Force, 7
aircraft
  British: Avro Lancaster, 59;
  Boulton Paul Defiant, 38;
  Bristol Beaufighter, 38, 105;
  Bristol Blenheim, 7, 38, 48,
  105; Fairey Battle, 7; Hawker
  Hurricane, 8, 9, 37, 38–40, 57,
  78, 80, 93, 95, 159–61; Vickers
  Supermarine Spitfire, 9,
  38–40, 57, 78, 80, 93, 95, 107,
  159–61;
  German: Dornier Do 17, 58;
  Heinkel He 111, 58; Heinkel
  He 113 (118), 58; Junkers Ju 87,
  58, 79; Junkers Ju 88, 59;

Messerschmitt Me 109 (Bf
  109), 51, 55, 56–7, 107, 122;
  Messerschmitt Me 110 (Bf
  110), 57–8;
  Soviet: I 16 fighter, 37
aircraft production, 36, 54–5, 125,
  127, 159
air fleets see German air fleets
air intelligence:
  American, 127
  British, 41, 115
  German, 78, 80, 106, 125, 126
Air Ministry (British), 3, 15, 33, 35,
  41, 50, 67, 70, 77, 84, 120, 130,
  131
air raids see bombing, Blitz
Alexander, General Harold, 129